DID YOU KNOW THAT . . .

- if you were born in the year of the Snake, you possess both the sensual intrigue of a Mata Hari and the wisdom of Confucius?

- people born under Earth signs make marvelous lovers?

- relationships between Fire and Metal people are destined to be explosive?

- people born in the year of the Sheep are known survivors? Never underestimate these resourceful and beguiling characters.

Now you can learn all there is to know about your personality, your strengths, your weaknesses, and your relationships with others—through Chinese elemental astrology, the oldest and most venerable system of astrology in the world.

E.A. CRAWFORD and TERESA KENNEDY also collaborated in the writing of *The Divination Handbook*, which is available in a Signet edition. They are both long-time students of Chinese astrology.

CHINESE ELEMENTAL
ASTROLOGY

by E.A. Crawford
and Teresa Kennedy

A SIGNET BOOK

SIGNET
Published by the Penguin Group
Penguin Books USA Inc., 375 Hudson Street,
New York, New York 10014, U.S.A.
Penguin Books Ltd, 27 Wrights Lane,
London W8 5TZ, England
Penguin Books Australia Ltd, Ringwood,
Victoria, Australia
Penguin Books Canada Ltd, 2801 John Street,
Markham, Ontario, Canada L3R 1B4
Penguin Books (N.Z.) Ltd, 182–190 Wairau Road,
Auckland 10, New Zealand

Penguin Books Ltd, Registered Offices:
Harmondsworth, Middlesex, England

First published by Signet, an imprint of New American Library,
a division of Penguin Books USA Inc.

First Printing, September, 1990
10 9 8 7 6 5 4 3 2 1

 REGISTERED TRADEMARK—MARCA REGISTRADA

PRINTED IN THE UNITED STATES OF AMERICA

BOOKS ARE AVAILABLE AT QUANTITY DISCOUNTS WHEN USED TO
PROMOTE PRODUCTS OR SERVICES. FOR INFORMATION PLEASE WRITE
TO PREMIUM MARKETING DIVISION, PENGUIN BOOKS USA INC., 375
HUDSON STREET, NEW YORK, NEW YORK 10014.

INTRODUCTION

A Brief History of the Chinese Astrological System

The art and practice of Chinese astrology, or *Ming Shu*, is believed to date from the year 2637 B.C., when the famous Yellow Emperor, Huang Ti, first introduced a calendar based on the cycles of the Moon. Literally translated, *Ming Shu* means "the reckoning of Fate," and this system has become the longest chronological record in history. Its companion science, Western astrology, is thought to have originated with the Babylonians, but in fact is based on the Oriental system that is many thousands of years older.

According to the Chinese system, the exact lunar year is determined by *T'ai sui*, which translates literally as the Great Year, and was thought by Chinese ancients to be an imaginary planet that travels through the heavens in a reverse course to the planet Jupiter. Its position in the heavens is believed to determine the dates of the Chinese calendar. The lunar year is divided into twelve months of 29 ½ days each, and each month begins on the day of the new moon. Every two and a half years, an extra month is added to adjust the calendar. The addition of this month every third year produces the Lunar Leap Year.

Unlike the twelve-month cycle of Western astrology, the Chinese cycle takes twelve *years* to complete. Each year is governed by an animal sign, which exerts a profound influence over the personality of an individual born in that year, much in the same way that Western personalities are thought to be governed by their zodiac sign.

But under the Chinese system, each lunar year is not only ruled by an animal, but by one of five elements, expressed in either a positive (Yang) manifestation or a negative (Yin) manifestation. The idea of the Five Elements is essential to many principals of Oriental thought and, simply put, states that all energy is expressed in five natural ways—through metal, water, wood, fire, or earth.

The five elements exert a profound influence over the individual chart that has been all but ignored in modern books on the subject. Most contemporary Western practitioners of Ming Shu have been content to add the obligatory statements on the elemental influences of the year of birth and seem to be more or less content to let it go at that. Yet tradition holds that in order to get a true picture of the individual's chart, personality, and even destiny the elemental forces of the date, time and hour of birth, and country of birth must also be considered and taken into account for the true elemental picture of the personality. Further, missing elements must be compensated for in home and working environments, as well as in personal relationships in order to provide for the individual's true development, happiness, and fulfillment.

This book will enable the reader to determine a personality profile based on his or her dominant element and will also show how to augment missing or lacking elements, balance positive and negative aspects, and discover which individuals are compatible with and sympathetic to his or her own personality. Keep in mind, though, that we have made adjustments for Western dates, times, and thinking in order to make the information and methods accessible to everyone. This book is meant to be enjoyed and used as a thorough and complete introduction to the practice of Chinese astrology. For further study, consult your local library or bookstore for literature on Feng Shui, the Chinese art of placement or energy enhancement in one's living environment, and Taoism in general. There are also many Taoist schools active in the United States, should the reader wish to continue these studies.

Chapter One

THE ANIMAL SIGNS

According to legend, the Lord Buddha summoned all the animals of the earth to him before he departed the world. Only twelve made the journey successfully, and in gratitude Buddha rewarded them by naming a year after them. The twelve years that resulted form the basis for the Chinese system.

In order to get any real understanding of Chinese astrology, it is important to "begin at the beginning." As significant as the elements and aspects are to anyone's chart, you must first identify your lunar sign by looking it up in Table 1-1, immediately following this chapter. "The animal that hides in your heart" exerts a profound influence upon your life, but remember as you read over the characteristics of your lunar sign that the connotations for specific animals differ greatly from West to East.

Westerners tend to think of snakes as untrustworthy, dangerous, and sinister, whereas Orientals view them as wise and honorable. Westerners consider the rat as a distasteful plague carrier, while Easterners regard this animal as highly social, practical, and hardworking. The horse is a beautiful, romantic animal in the occidental mind, while Orientals consider this animal to be unfortunately headstrong, willful, difficult to control. As a matter of fact, to be born under the sign of the horse in a year when the element of fire dominates is considered in the Chinese system singularly tragic, even to the point where Chinese mothers have opted for voluntary abortions as an alternative to bringing a child so afflicted into the world!

The dragon, a mythical adversary in Western legends, is viewed by Orientals as the epitome of style. To the Easterner, the sheep is sensitive and artistic, while the Westerner views sheep as docile and somewhat stupid! The rabbit symbolizes fertility and rebirth in Western thinking, but the Chinese consider them somewhat devious, despite a certain amount of natural luck. A person born in the Year of the Ox might be viewed by the Westerner as boring and slow, but in the Chinese system the ox is patient, constant, and honorable—possessed of great strength. The Westerner would tame or slay the tiger, but the Easterner views the wildness of the tiger as sensual, vivacious, and oddly placid within the context of long-term relationships. Monkeys are cute and entertaining to the Westerner and difficult to take seriously, but the Easterner finds them resourceful, clever, somewhat vain, and capable of deceit. Interestingly enough, the United States was "born" in the Year of the Monkey, which makes the Easterner always a little suspicious of American motives! The Oriental considers the rooster to be fault-finding and critical to the point of pettiness, while the Westerner would view the rooster as a leader and communicator. The dog is friendly, loyal, and faithful in Occidental thought, whereas the Oriental finds this creature a fierce and aggressive fighter, and a champion for the causes of others. The boar connotes laziness and sloth to the Westerner, but to the Eastern mind the boar is pleasure-seeking and gifted with great money-making powers.

To get a more comprehensive idea of the differences between the Oriental and Occidental views of the animal signs, it may be helpful for you to do some additional research into Oriental folklore. Eastern folk tales and fables are filled with anthropomorphic references that can be fascinating and entertaining, even to the casual reader.

Again, keep in mind that a person's animal sign is only one of the determining factors in a person's chart, and can be very significantly altered by the attendant elements and aspects.

The Animal Signs

The Rat

Associated with the Western astrological sign of Sagittarius, the Rat is ruled by the planet Jupiter. Its direction is north and it rules the hours of 11

P.M. to 1 A.M. Rats born in the daytime hours during the summer have an easier path in life than those born in the nighttime hours of winter.

A cool, possessed, social personality, whose house is always overflowing with distant relatives, friends, and strays, and whose cupboards are stacked with all manner of sundries and supplies bought at discount is almost certainly a Rat. On closer inspection, his or her disarming manner will give way to signs of an almost inexhaustible nervous energy. Toe-tapping, fingernail biting, facial tics, and restless movements of all kinds characterize this person. To say nothing of the fact that all those apparent freeloaders in the Rat's household are almost certainly earning their keep. If you have an aversion to hard work, you ought to think twice about accepting the Rat's legendary charity.

Rats are almost always ambitious and surrounded by a close-knit group of equally ambitious friends. They not only know what they want, but they know how to get it. One of the most practical of all of the signs, the Rat has an enormous capacity for work and a remarkable ability to enlist the support of others. Not only that, but they have a highly developed instinct for self-preservation. If you suspect you are in trouble, watch the Rat to see what he does. Conversely, the Rat's best quality, his ambition, can also be his worst flaw. He is capable of scattering his energies and not completing tasks. As good as his judgment is, he often fails to follow it because of sentimental reasons.

Another distinguishing characteristic of the Rat is frugality. He values money, knows how to make it, and will go to astonishing lengths to keep it. Money represents security to the native of the Rat year. In more afflicted aspects, this quality can disintigrate into miserliness and unremitting greed. Still, the Rat wastes nothing. Under some circumstances, he can be extraordinarily generous, providing that he loves the person or people involved.

The Rat in love, for example, spends with wild abandon and often embarrassing generosity on the loved one. If you capture the heart of the Rat, prepare to be treated very well. Rats are inveterate collectors and will loosen their purse strings for books, objets d'art, stamps, antiques, and other collectibles—all of which will clutter their homes. Rat collections have investment value in theory, but practically the Rat never parts with anything, even if he is starving.

The Rat also spends unlimited amounts of money to further his ambitions. Take a look at career development courses and expense reports. He may spend $80 to redesign an old suit rather than buy a new one and turn around and invest $250 on someone who will promote him. Rats make excellent business people, writers, historians, and troubleshooters of all kinds because of their eye for detail. Nuances in facts and figures rarely escape their attention. These people have the ability to cope with almost any difficulty and are at their best in a crisis. They are excellent at running homes, corporations, and handling other people's money.

Emotions and Relationships

On the surface, Rats may appear to be reserved. In fact, they may be so adept at concealing their feelings that they find it hard to communicate their emotions to others, even when they want to. The Rat is never as quiet as he looks. He is impressionable, easily agitated, and eternally curious. Within the context of family and trusted friends, the rat can be very sociable. But the Rat can't rid himself of strong emotional attachments with any more ease than he can his possessions. His capacity to love is exceeded only by his capacity for work. Rat charm can conceal selfishness and possessiveness when it comes to those he loves. Rats dote on their families and are particularly close to children and parents. They hide their own secrets well, because they are superb at getting others to reveal their innermost thoughts. To the Rat, talking about another person's problems is always preferable to talking about himself. The Rat isn't adverse to using the information he has culled to his own advantage.

Compatibility

The Rat is naturally attracted to the hard-working Ox, the loyal Dragon, and the security-conscious Snake. He delights in the versatility and scams of the Monkey and can have successful relationships with the Tiger, the Boar, or another Rat. Rats and Horses rarely get along unless there are mitigating features in the charts of the individuals involved. The Horse is too changeable and "selfish" for the clannish, conservative Rat. Alliances with Roosters are equally unwise: They are too dramatic and impractical for the Rat, who can see through their act and need for affection. Sheep will spend the Rat's money on frivolities and the Rat may suspect the Sheep will treat his affections with an equally open-handed aplomb.

The Ox

The hours ruled by the Ox are 1 A.M. to 3 A.M. This sign corresponds to the Western sign of Capricorn. The Ox is ruled by Saturn and its direction is north-northeast. The winter Ox will have a harder life than one born during the summer. Oxen born at night are quieter and less aggressive than their day-born sisters and brothers.

Some of the best things in life come in plain packages; the Ox is one of them. The quiet-eyed person whose gentleness is surprising in the face of what he has endured is sure to be an Ox. Ox people have an almost supernatural patience and dependability. They are calm, methodical, and dutiful. They repay debts, sometimes years later, and never forget a favor (or disfavor) done them. Oxen can be depended upon to speak softly and haul around a big stick. Sometimes they are unfairly criticized for lack of imagination, but this is not necessarily the case. They like to use intelligence and dexterity as a foil to their calm, undemonstrative front. Their minds like logic, which they combine to good effect with their reliability and industriousness. But as conventional as the Ox may seem, public opinion means almost nothing to this person. He couldn't care less what other people think, say, or do. Perhaps because of this, he goes through life almost untroubled and this gives him a peculiar kind of independence that makes other, more sensitive signs wonder where he has hid his head all those years. He is unaffected by fashion or trends.

Highly materialistic, the Ox is capable of great sacrifices on emotional, physical, and material levels and will never let you down. He doesn't give his word lightly but once he has, that promise will be kept. Oxen have a strong personal morality and will never resort to cunning, deceit, or unfair means to achieve their goals. Conscientious to a fault, the Ox builds things to last. These people quietly construct empires and dynasties with dignity while the flightier of the Animal signs cruise the most current watering spots. They build families with the same thought to permanence and are not above pontificating around the dinner table. These are people who tell favorite jokes and stories many times over. The Ox succeeds easily in the military because of his imperviousness to pain, in the law because of his painstaking ability to come to a fair solution, in banking because he can be trusted with investment, and in insurance because it is a long-term solution to the vagaries of life's fickleness.

Emotions and Relationships

Although the Ox rarely experiences love at first sight, it is a mistake to assume he is not passionate and capable of deep, intense emotion. The Ox is perennially innocent and can be terribly naive about affairs of the heart. Never much of a strategist, the intricacies of romantic entrapment, lyric poetry, and inspired courtship are a little beyond him. He is slow to warm up and slow to reveal his true feelings. Once his heart is given, though, it is for all time. It is rare for him to be unfaithful and his love grows over the years.

Charging Oxen are rarely an attractive sight. The Ox may lose his temper once in thirty years but when he does, it is impressive, more like an atomic war than a simple display of fireworks. When he manages to calm down, rest assured he will hold a grudge. The Ox nurtures grievances until death and does not hesitate to recount injuries (real and imagined) in excruciating detail. If the Ox is severely disappointed in a relationship, it is not unusual for him to bury himself in work and choose a solitary life rather than run the risk of another betrayal. For all of his strength, resilience and adaptability are not Ox traits. However big the Oxen heart, it is slow to love and even slower to heal.

Compatibility

The best match for the Ox is the Rooster. Both respect authority, work efficiently, and possess dedicated personalities. The deeply affectionate Rat and Snake make good matches for the deserving Ox. The Dog-born find Oxen boring and criticize the Ox for lacking a sense of humor. Oxen find Sheep people fickle in love and at all costs should stay away from their natural enemy, the Tiger.

The Tiger

The sign of the Tiger corresponds to the Western sign of Aquarius and is ruled by Uranus. The hours for this sign are 3 A.M. to 5 A.M., and its direction is east-northeast.

A Tiger in your house may be hard to live with, but he is guaranteed to ward off fire, thieves, and ghosts, long considered by Orientals to be the three principal disasters of a household. Movie legend Bruce Lee is considered to be the quintessential Tiger. The Tiger's recklessness is matched only by his love of life. The one thing the Tiger is not likely to inspire is indifference, but that is just as well, because the one thing the Tiger requires of the world is to bask in the limelight and be the center of attention.

This sign's natural response to his suspicions of the world around him is to make hasty, reckless decisions. Nevertheless, he is as sincere, affectionate, and generous as he is quick-tempered and daring. And any scratch you might receive from the Tiger can usually be healed by his overwhelming sense of humor and considerable genuine charm. Rebellious and easily frustrated, the Tiger gives 100 percent of himself in reaching for whatever goal happens to be in his sights at the moment. These people are the ultimate optimists, but they do need to guard against indecision and combustibility—a tendency to burn out. Frequently the Tiger believes that any decision is better than no decision at all, but that is perhaps only a reaction to his never-ending capacity to see all sides of an issue. If he can manage, to balance his impulsiveness and indecision with a modicum of patience and foresight, however, success is almost always assured.

Tigers have a bohemian streak and can be quite unconventional when it comes to taking risks and breaking rules. Whatever else the Tiger is, he is never dull. They tend, for all their unpredictability, to be surprisingly successful in money and career matters, but the road to success for the Tiger is never without its pitfalls and potholes. Although they can seem annoyingly selfish and fickle to the observer, the Tiger is a diehard humanitarian at heart. He almost always has a distinct personal style and does well in fashion, acting, daredevil sports such as stunt work and race-car driving, and public entertainment professions of all kinds. They are the types of people who are constantly reinventing themselves, and are quite capable of conning the dubious. Highly verbal, Tigers always let you know what's on their mind at the moment, and even if it's best to view them with a little healthy skepticism, they will doubtless make life more exciting.

Emotions and Relationships

Depressed Tigers need unlimited and unconditional sympathy; they don't want to hear about who is right and who is wrong. Any advice you offer the Tiger will ultimately be disregarded once the smoke clears, but he will be grateful that you took the time to offer it anyway. A shattered ego is the worst blow a Tiger can suffer, so kick back, listen, and let him pour out his troubles until he's ready to tackle the world once again. Capable of mind-boggling mood swings, the tiger can exhibit some truly manic moments, but no matter how great his emotional destruction, he always bounces back. The stress of his own personality can render the Tiger obstinate, unreasonable, and entirely too intense for more ordinary mortals. They are not negotiators and have a kind of "all-or-nothing" approach to getting what they want from life. If they have a principal flaw, it is quite possibly their capacity for vengeance; once crossed, the Tiger will stop at nothing, up to and including his own destruction, to get revenge. And yet, paradoxically, they can allow major issues or problems in a relationship to pass all but unnoticed—as long as the Tiger is not ignored.

Tigers are sensual and, surprise! highly emotional. They enjoy love wherever they find it and may be highly indiscriminate about just where they find it. Older, more settled Tigers are devoted to their mates and although highly unpredictable, are unlikely to stray. All Tigers adore children and can make them toe the line, if not through quiet reasoning, then by charm and a kind of awesome authority.

Compatibility

Tigers are compatible with Horses. Both love activity and living life to the fullest. To say nothing of the fact that the Horse is better at sensing danger than the more scattered Tiger. The Boar provides him with security; practical, fun-loving Dogs are also a good match. Dogs are probably the only Animal sign capable of reasoning with the Tiger. Rats, Sheep, and Roosters combine well with the Tiger, as do other Tigers, although that relationship is sure to be strenuous. About all the extravagant Tiger and the cool, collected Snake have in common is an equally suspicious view of the world. In the Tiger, this expresses itself in rash accusation, but the ways of the Snake are cold and calculated. They never find harmony. The Monkey has no defense but to deceive the Tiger with its clever ways, whereas the rebelliousness of the tiger is sure to enrage the Ox. In a contest like that, the Tiger always loses.

The Rabbit

The sign of the Rabbit corresponds to the Western astrological sign of Pisces, and rules the hours of 5 A.M. to 7 A.M. Its direction is east, and its planetary ruler is Neptune. Rabbits born in the summer are more fortunate than those born in the winter.

*   *   *

Rabbits love peace more than anything else in the world. They are sensitive to the interests of others; they are artistic and are among the luckiest of the Animal signs. Rabbits are formidable negotiators, perhaps because they loathe a good fight. Diplomatic and kind, they can nevertheless be ruthless when they feel that their interests are in jeopardy. Rabbits can appear to be slow or inordinately timid at times, but should they have to fight, they do so with courage and determination. The outward docility of the Rabbit can be misleading; because of their strong wills and suave self-assurance they can at times appear vain and self-involved.

Rabbits are difficult to read successfully; it is almost always hard to know what they are really thinking. Impeccable manners, graciousness, and self-indulgence often deceive others into thinking they are lazy or hedonistic. This is rarely the case.

In Chinese mythology, the Rabbit is a symbol for longevity. Rabbits frequently live long and very comfortable lives because of their innate dislike of placing themselves in dangerous circumstances and an almost magical sense of self-preservation. When given a choice, the Rabbit opts for comfort every time. Their inner balance and conformity keep them from being trendy, flashy, or aggressive. Although they may let these characteristics pass in others, they consider them theoretically distasteful. Not easily trapped, the Rabbit is an expert at passing the buck. They dislike ironclad commitments and overinvolvement, and can be very secretive about their private lives. But their love of the good life is not purely self-indulgent. These people genuinely appreciate beauty, adore the arts and, if not creatively inclined themselves, make wonderful philanthropists, patrons, and critics.

As the most fortunate of all signs in the Chinese cycle, the Rabbit is more likely to achieve happiness and contentment than other Animal signs. Naturally elegant and aristocratic, he is superb at handling stress. He is convinced it takes little for people to be kind to each other. But Rabbit natives value themselves above all else. This is not a person who readily risks security and comfort for others or even the good of the whole unless pushed to the wall, in which case the Rabbit negotiates a solution beneficial to all, particularly the underdog, rather than embark on a messy, noisy fight. The Rabbit is a gentleman in the nineteenth-century sense of the word. *Noblesse oblige* is inborn in his personality and he can be counted upon to display grace under pressure.

The Rabbit has an unerring eye for quality, and for this reason they make good art collectors and dealers. Rabbits in business will pursue personal objectives with an elegant precision. If you just let your Ming vase go to that utterly charming individual who knew just how to treat you, or signed a contract (the terms of which weren't *exactly* what you wanted), you can be sure you've fallen victim to the cunning of the Hare. What is dangerous about the Rabbit is that his methods are so utterly painless. You won't know what hit you and, chances are, you will become his friend.

Rabbit personalities can range from people like Joseph Stalin and Fidel Castro to Albert Einstein, Queen Victoria, and David Rockefeller. At best, the Rabbit is debonair, intelligent, and sensible. At worst, he is oversensitive and indifferent, the kind of person who avoids human suffering as though it were some kind of contagious disease. Even Rabbits with no money surround themselves with a mental dream world that protects them from the harsher realities of life.

Emotions and Relationships

Sensual and fond of physical pleasure, the Rabbit nevertheless rarely enters into a relationship with someone incapable of contributing to his comfort, ease, or status in the world. Capable of great mood swings that others find disconcerting, the Rabbit can also demonstrate a talent for deception, which is generally triggered by his dislike of confrontational situations. Rabbits are evasive; they are not above saying just what others want to hear. When reproached or challenged, expect nothing more from the Rabbit than a cool, philosophical indifference and maddening calm. The phrase, "That would be a *frightful* bore," was undoubtedly invented by a Rabbit native.

Although Rabbits are oddly estranged from their immediate families, they always provide. They are more likely to send off a sizable check to the folks back home than pick up the telephone. Socially, Rabbits have a good word to say about everyone. Don't let that fool you. They are marvelous friends and wonderful lovers as long as you don't expect too much from them. Nevertheless the Rabbit is elegant, graceful, and highly romantic, especially when he or she is amply provided for.

Compatibility

The Sheep is perhaps the best match for the inscrutable Rabbit; both share innate good taste and love of luxury. Relationships with the loyal Dog or pleasure-seeking Boar are often happy and productive. It is said that Rabbits and Snakes are the stuff legendary love affairs are made of, although these lovers may baffle those around them. Tigers and Rabbits rarely get along—they understand each other too well. Relationships with the unruly Horse and devious Monkey can also be difficult. Rabbits prefer tranquillity to careening off in twelve directions. Peace-loving and flexible, the Rabbit gets along well with the Rat, Dragon, and Ox. Relationships with other Rabbits are not passionate, but they can nevertheless be very compatible if allowed separate spheres of influence. On no account should they attempt serious involvement with the brash Rooster. The abrasive criticism of this sign will send a Rabbit running into permanent hiding.

The Dragon

The sign of the Dragon corresponds to the Western astrological sign of Aries and rules the hours of 7 A.M. to 9 A.M. Its planetary ruler is Mars and direction is east-southeast. Spring and summer Dragons are more powerful than fall and winter Dragons.

Those born under the sign of the Dragon are said to wear the horns of destiny. No other sign represents power like the Dragon. Energy, egotism, and eccentricity are all characteristics of the Dragon born, the zealots of the Chinese calendar. Eager and enthusiastic, the Dragon represents energy in all of its forms. Chinese mythology tells us that the strong energy lines that influence the atmosphere of the earth's crust are due to the flight of the Dragon. Visionary and proud, Dragons are nevertheless peculiarly guileless. That's because they are usually moving too fast to be bothered with anything as complex as a lie. They are equally incapable of discerning deceit or cunning in other people. The Chinese consider those born in the Year of the Dragon to have all the qualities of an emperor. This belief prompts many couples to marry in the Year of the Rabbit to ensure that their firstborn will be a Dragon child.

Possessed of enormous potential, it is difficult to find an unsuccessful Dragon. They lead magically protected lives. Never petty, they are marked by an astonishing generosity. Still, there is often a loner element lurking in the soul of the Dragon. They do not make friends easily, although they can form good and powerful relationships that are always sincere, at least on their part.

The Dragon is sure to rush into those numerous places where even angels fear to tread. They make the best warriors and are untiring opponents, fueled as they are by the inner fire of their convictions. Their unshakable belief in themselves can border on the arrogant and domineering. These are people possessed of almost superhuman integrity—they are convinced that they arrived in the world to raise standards in whatever arena they decide to inhabit. Although the Dragon is entrepreneurial and pioneering, his road to fortune is sure to be marked by both great success and spectacular failure.

No-nonsense types, Dragons live by the bottom line. They proceed in a straight path toward their goals and never go in circles. Above all else, the Dragon needs something to *do*. Activity is everything. A Dragon who lies around languishing is not a healthy Dragon.

Dragons are almost always surrounded by crowds of adoring admirers. The average Dragon is, however, completely unconscious of his own magnetism. While it is rare to find a Dragon without a large and healthy ego, he is more inclined to view the world as a whole, rather than as a stage on which he is playing the leading role. Though he is capable of a detached analysis of a particular problem, when it comes to a solution, the Dragon is not above championing his own cause—and Dragons often have many causes to champion.

Because of his great magnetism, the only profession suitable for the Dragon is that of leader. Dragons are dazzling, not decorative.

Natural extroverts, Dragons are excellent talkers and can sell anyone anything. The integrity and charisma of this individual lend a credibility to whatever he is promoting at the moment. Blessed with resilience, a Dragon is never be down for long.

Emotions and Relationships

If peace and security are what you seek, stay away from the Dragon. He is the adventurer *extraordinaire*. When he tells you he loves you, you can be assured that he is telling the truth. But the truth, as any Dragon knows, can change. Dragons often fall in love for life at an early age. Despite their natural tendency to solitude, Dragons marry young or not at all. Emotionally intense, a Dragon native prefers to be needed as well as loved.

Whatever you do, don't laugh at a Dragon, even when he turns the simplest things into high ritual. And do remember, when a Dragon confides his dreams of greatness, he isn't just whistling in the dark. Take him seriously. He believes it. You should too.

Even in the context of a relationship, the Dragon needs to feel useful. His heart can only be broken if his ego is bruised first. Once you have won the heart of Dragons they are loyal beyond belief. As a matter of fact, the only real crime of the heart that can be committed against a Dragon is to prove yourself unworthy of his devotion. These people put their loved ones on a pedestal.

Not particularly close to their families, Dragons plunge into the world at an early age. They do, however, appreciate children because of the promise of the future vested in small human beings.

Compatibility

The Dragon makes the best match with the irresistible Monkey because he is drawn to Monkey charm and cleverness. Monkeys do well to pair up with the Dragon; no matter how intriguing, integrity is not necessarily a Monkey forte unless there are mitigating influences in the chart. Dragons provide drama and add stability to the crafty business sense of the Rat. Snakes and Dragons appreciate each other. Snakes provide restraint and levelheadedness in a way that can keep the natural Dragon excessiveness in check. All signs seek out the Dragon for his beauty and strength. Surprisingly, even two Dragons can get along well. Oxen are too methodical and Dogs should be avoided at all counts because, with their intellect and cynicism, they tend to snap at the Dragon's wings.

The Snake

Snakes correspond to the Western sign of Taurus. This sign rules the hours of 9 A.M. to 11 A.M. Governed by Venus, the direction of the sign is south-southeast. Spring and summer Snakes are deadly, but Snake natives born in the cooler months are generally docile and calm.

Snakes combine the sensual intrigue of a Mata Hari with the wisdom of Confucius. Snakes are often psychically inclined, deeply religious, or even downright mystical. They are not, however, ascetics. The Snake has a wide and potent hedonistic streak that expresses itself in a love of luxury and beauty. You will never find a Snake living on a diet of brown rice and raw vegetables; they love good food and wine. If you can't come up with the best, they would prefer to do without, thank you.

The power and beauty of the Snake is exceeded only by his cool charisma and wily intelligence. Interestingly enough, Snake people often have some difficulty communicating with others. Like its preceding sign, the Dragon, the Snake is very good at attracting and making money. But unlike the Dragon, the Rabbit, or the Monkey, the Snake should avoid gambling and speculation. Snakes are suspicious by nature, and have a curious, deadly-accurate intuition about the motives of others. But rest assured this will never express itself in wild accusation or mere paranoia. The Snake always chooses the most precise, advantageous moment to strike.

Snake natives frequently harbor their share of dark secrets, but these are rarely as interesting as the kind of speculation they can generate in others. Mysterious and even remote at times, the Snake is not one to tip his hand. Loaded with sex appeal and discretion, they exude a dramatic air of mystery. When a Snake enters a room, people always notice that he or she is there. Cinderella was most certainly a Snake.

Snakes are seemingly impervious to ordinary kinds of upsets and even disasters, probably because they are continually in tune with that deeper philosophical knowledge of the world and how it works. They surround themselves with those whom they are sure will live up to their standards—the rest of the rabble doesn't concern them. They can be possessive and jealous, but they do value their associates. Nevertheless, Snakes have long and vivid memories, they are not forgiving by nature and are simply not the kind to let a misdeed or betrayal go unpunished.

Oddly, the Snake's initial reaction to stress or crisis usually expresses itself in a wry and sometimes almost perverse sense of humor. It won't be until later that the Snake begins to exact his revenge. They rarely have patience for the shallower types, and can move easily and naturally in circles of power. They will overcome astonishing obstacles in order to achieve what they want for themselves and their loved ones. It is rare to find a Snake at the bottom of the heap, but this sign does tend to extremes. In a way, the Snake is a sign of "instant Karma." The Chinese believe that the Snake is one sign who must, by hook or by crook, resolve any Karmic problems within the span of his lifetime.

If the Snake's considerable intellect should express itself in a creative fashion, he or she will produce works that will endure. The Snake's inner philosphical connections are expressed in artforms with near-archetypal appeal. Although the Snake can appear to be languid, his brain never stops. Snakes make wonderful politicians, actors and religious leaders.

Emotions and Relationships

The phrase, "Still waters run deep" was almost certainly invented to describe the Snake. Snakes are passionate underneath their serene exteriors, but they rarely allow their true feelings to show. When they do, you can be sure the show was well planned in advance. They protect and nurture those they love and establish long and binding friendships. They are passionate lovers because of their sensual natures. They appreciate difficult people and are capable of maintaining complex relationships. The average snake is frequently perceived as having all sorts of intrigues and liaisons underway, which may or may not be the case. They are excellent and wise advisers, and are very good at solving others' problems—when they deign to be involved. The Snake is one of the most adept seducers of the Chinese calendar, but will rarely undertake such seductions lightly. They are naturally sophisticated, oddly responsible, and can excel in adversity. The Snake gravitates unerringly toward the real sources of prestige and power in any society, whether or not those sources are apparent to anyone else. Because they are sensitive and high-strung, they have a predilection for nervous disorders.

Compatibility

The machinations and calculations of the Snake will further the causes of the Ox and Rooster, but Snakes are at their best when mated with the Dragon, the Rabbit or the Sheep—all signs that tend to move in powerful, elite circles. Snakes can get along with almost any Animal sign, even when they appear to have little in common. Exceptions to this are the Tiger, the Horse, and the Monkey. The Boar and the Snake do not understand each other, because they are so completely opposite in disposition and inclination.

The Horse

The Horse corresponds to the Western Zodiac sign of Gemini, and rules the hours of 11 A.M. and 1 P.M. Its direction is south, its ruling planet, Mercury. Summer Horses lead a more secure and less temperamental existence than winter Horses, but Horses are never truly comfortable until well into middle age.

Horses are cheerful, freedom-loving, and almost always irresistible. Liberty, but not necessarily the liberty of others, is the motivating force for those born under the sign of the Horse. Horse independence often inconveniences others, because it is all but impossible for any Horse native to adhere to a schedule or timetable. They keep odd hours and can become insomniacs if they don't succeed in wearing themselves out before attempting to sleep. Although easily flattered, the Horse is highly perceptive and a phenomenally fast thinker; he can draw conclusions about people and situations based on the flimsiest of evidence. Occasionally, the Horse will depend entirely too much on his intuition and jump to improbable, impulsive conclusions, but he is responsible enough to live with the consequences. Horses are not possessive, suspicious, or jealous, and they can talk anybody into anything. They are easily frustrated when they find that others simply don't have the capacity to turn on a dime the way they can. The Horse loves action; he talks fast, he thinks fast, and he moves fast, but the Horse is not necessarily in it for the long haul.

Physical exercise is of the utmost importance for the Horse and exertions tend to calm his highstrung nature. The Horse is full of contradictions; he is the kind who will work for a thirty-six-hour stretch and cannot be dragged from his bed for the next twenty! Flexible and versatile, when a Horse encounters the winds of change, he is likely to adroitly sidestep the weather and come back again another day. Like the Western sign of Gemini, the Horse is a busy sign. They can answer their phones, type a letter, and eat lunch all at the same time.

Horse natives, however, can be fickle. They require travel and variety to remain at their peak, and need the respites of nature to calm them down. They make excellent salespeople, reporters, actors, and communicators of all kinds. What they have in communication skills, however, they tend to lack in patience. They make poor teachers and homemakers, and anything that requires routine is deadly to the restless Horse. Excitable and even frantic at times, the Horse is not the person to seek out in times of crisis. Anxious as he may be to help, he'll probably only succeed in making the situation worse than it is, and exhaust you as well. While the Horse is never intentionally deceptive, he is not above a few dramatics and can stretch the truth in an attempt to color the world according to his own imaginative viewpoint. If you're waiting for the bottom line, don't expect to hear it from the Horse's mouth. Oddly enough, however, the Horse expects you to come to the point as quickly as possible. He has a short attention span, and little time for those who hem and haw their way to the issue.

Emotions and Relationships

Horses are well liked by nearly everybody and have a large circle of friends—but they can strain their friendships beyond belief. Not only are they moody, but they have violent, if short-lived explosions of temper. To make the situation worse, the Horse expects you to forgive as easily as he does and has little patience for anyone petty enough to hold a grudge or nurse wounded feelings for long. They are eccentric but have great personal strength, perhaps due to their flexibility. Generous with their time, money, and personal resources, the Horse will always bolt if his freedom is threatened. Security is unimportant to them. They are rarely attached to home and family; Horses always leave home early. Although they are capable of loyalty and devotion to spouses and children, settling down in order get those things is not easy for the Horse. They expect others to forgive their transgressions and emotional wanderings as easily as they themselves forget them.

Compatibility

Horses form the best partnerships with Tigers, Dogs, and Sheep. The Dog will keep the recklessness of the Horse in check, and Tigers will stimulate their restless minds. The Horse feels protective of the Sheep, who does not mind the inconsistencies of the Horse's behavior and lifestyle. The Horse has a finely tuned sense of danger and can provide excellent advice and counsel to the fiercer Dragon. Horses get along well with Snakes, Monkeys, Rabbits, Boars, Roosters, and other Horses, because the natives of these signs never place limits on any of the horse's freedom. Rats and Horses suspect each other's motives, and the Ox is far too methodical and rigid for any Horse to deal with for any length of time. Conversely, the Ox is in it for the long haul and characteristically whimsical Horse behavior will cause any self-respecting Ox to break out in hives.

The Sheep

The sign of the Sheep corresponds to the Western sign of Cancer, and its planetary ruler is the Moon. It rules the hours of 1 P.M. to 3 P.M., and its direction is south-southwest. Winter sheep are thought to have a harder time in life than summer sheep.

Sheep are the most altruistic sign of the Chinese cycle. Truly good Samaritans, Sheep are easily recognized by their gentle and compassionate ways. Shy and sincere, the Sheep gives the impression of being very mild-mannered. His sympathy for the troubles of the less fortunate can be exploited by those less scrupulous than the worthy Sheep.

Supersensitive, Sheep can react quite badly to any form of personal criticism, and the mildest rebuke can send them into a positive orgy of self-doubt and hopeless pessimism. For this reason, the Sheep can give the impression of being moody and withdrawn, though this is not usually the case at all. As easy as he is to hurt, the gentle Sheep is just as quick to forgive. The moody side of the Sheep is not so much pessimism as it is worry. Sheep worry about everything—themselves, their friends, world problems; the term *bleeding heart* must have been originally coined with the Sheep in mind.

Yet it is a mistake to think that the Sheep is just another pushover. Like the Rabbit, the Sheep's approach to getting what he wants out of life is more oblique than some of the other signs, but not necessarily less effective. The Sheep is a survivor—he has an infallible instinct for knowing how to placate his enemies. Watch the Sheep in action sometime; he has a great, nearly magical talent for turning his apparent weaknesses to his own advantage. Never underestimate the beguiling Sheep; he is quite capable of manipulating others through insinuation and subtlety and can be extremely patient. This is a sign that is long-suffering and capable of great passive endurance, but you will never know just how strong the Sheep can be until you try to break him. Though he hates a fight, when attacked he can respond passionately. When actually angered—truly a rare event—he can turn into a crazed warrior.

Considered one of the more fortunate signs, the Sheep, it is said, will never have to work very hard—perhaps because the Sheep can be so good at getting others to take care of him. Nevertheless, they have a great appreciation of not only creature comforts but the finer things, and within the Sheep is the soul of an aristocrat. Never selfish, he is as generous with others as he expects others to be with him and has a refreshing, easygoing approach to grittier financial matters. Career wise, it is not so important what the Sheep does as who surrounds him when he does it. Sheep can benefit greatly from the influence of strong associates. Sheep are comforting people to be around when their friends are in trouble. Warm-hearted and sympathetic, a Sheep will listen and sympathize and often come up with good advice, if not actual nuts-and-bolts solutions to concrete problems. Sheep are tranquil sorts, good people to have around in between battles with the world at large.

Emotions and Relationships

Sheep are hopeless romantics. They are deeply tied to home and family, and remain close to parents and siblings. No Sheep can ever manage to forget a birthday or anniversary. It is difficult for Sheep to cut apron strings once they have been securely tied. Because they are moody, emotional, and sensitive, Sheep get little satisfaction out of being blunt. They can give friends the silent treatment, lapse into prolonged pouts, and indulge in theatrics. Humor them or leave them alone; Sheep do quite well on their own. They also respond well to heavy doses of sympathy and can always be coaxed back into good humor with promises and rewards.

Conversely, Sheep are unimpressed with displays of anger and temperament; besides seeing right through them, Sheep are docile creatures and prefer tranquil associates. Quiet strength, patience, and a winning smile are sure ways to win the heart of a Sheep.

Compatibility

The Sheep does best surrounded with those who are stronger, more direct, and even more bad-tempered than he. Sheep partners must compliment these shy creatures rather than resemble them. The extroverted, optimistic Horse is the perfect foil to the sensitive Sheep. Rabbits and Sheep are highly compatible and make the best of friends. They understand each other on a deep intuitive level. The versatile Monkey, the fiery Dragon, and the eccentric Rooster all make satisfactory associations. Oxen lack sensitivity to fully appreciate the sentimental Sheep. Thrifty Rats will fight with Sheep over money, much to the Sheep's surprise. Dogs have no patience with seemingly endless Sheep woes and moodiness. Oddly, two Sheep can sometimes combine their apparent weaknesses into a strongly united front.

The Monkey

The Monkey corresponds to the Western astrological sign of Leo. It rules the hours of 3 P.M. to 5 P.M. and is ruled by the Sun. Its direction is west-southwest, and it is thought that summer Monkeys are more straightforward and less naturally devious and mischievous than their winter brothers and sisters.

Monkeys are gamblers, speculators, and risk-takers. Impish and inventive, they have great power to inspire and and motivate others, assuming that power is not frittered away in mere quantity, rather than quality of pursuits. The Monkey born are never at a loss for words, solutions, or jokes. They are the most adaptable sign of all the animals, and are more than likely to speak a number of languages—either in an actual or metaphorical sense. Versatile and quick-witted, they will move with ease through any number of circles. They can get themselves into and out of more messes than almost anyone else, probably because it is difficult to be angry with a Monkey for very long.

Although it is hard to trust the Monkey at times, he is never too concerned with the opinions of others—perhaps because he rarely hangs around long enough to find out what those opinions may be, much less to take them to heart. Charming and quick-witted, the Monkey has little patience for slower types. One thing the Monkey is never without is great confidence in himself and his own abilities. In fact, badly aspected Monkeys can succumb to vanity and be extremely self-serving. Highly ingenious, Monkeys invariably use that ability to get the best out of whatever deal happens to be on the table at the moment. But when (and if!) the Monkey's conscience asserts itself, he will be warm-hearted and generous with whomever he meets.

For all of his playfulness, the Monkey is an intellectual and shrewd at judging others. They have a practical streak as wide as a superhighway, and it is rare to find a Monkey doing without. Independent in the extreme, when cornered, the Monkey will make for the nearest exit and be off, pursuing any one of a number of alternative plans. Warm, natural, and spontaneous, the Monkey nevertheless has a great sense of fair play and will be angry if anyone is so bold as to try and dupe or deceive him.

He doesn't care to discuss his troubles or to get overly personal and the triumphs and pitfalls of others make little impression on him—his attention span is simply too short. Monkeys solve problems as easily as they play and are marked by a devastatingly sharp sense of humor. Never try to fool the Monkey; he is more shrewd than you are. Highly competitive and insatiably curious, the Monkey is interested in everything. They have a great talent for making and investing money, probably because they are attracted by the gamesmanship of high finance. They make excellent critics, actors, stockbrokers, lawyers, and diplomats. They can also excel as writers, assuming that they can muster the personal discipline. But whatever profession the Monkey chooses, he is at his best when breaking, or at least stretching, the rules.

Emotions and Relationships

Monkeys are happy-go-lucky people; it simply does no good to yell at them. Criticism rolls off their backs. Even worse, they will probably ridicule you for making the effort! The Monkey is often misunderstood as being shallow and lacking in serious purpose, but even that does not trouble him. If you can't keep up, says the Monkey, you don't get to play. The Monkey is an expert at getting you to pour out your heart's secrets, but don't expect much by way of reciprocity—the Monkey doesn't like the "touchy-feely" side of things. Monkeys pull themselves back from the brink just when you're sure they are going to tumble off into oblivion or that their luck has finally run out. Highly adroit, they can readjust and rebalance in the blinking of an eye. Monkeys lie cheerfully to help their friends, sometimes with disastrous results. Badly aspected, the monkey's mental agility can turn snobbish and critical and he will prove all but impossible to get close to. Monkeys prefer friendly, stimulating relationships to passionate liaisons. They like and are curious about everyone, but do have difficulty narrowing the field. Once a little more settled, though, they can prove loyal and devoted, if not highly emotional. Of all the signs, they are the best with children.

Compatibility

Monkeys and rats get along very well because they both share a love of problem solving and money making. Dragons love their intelligence, and the Monkey's playful approach can provide an excellent foil for the Dragon's more direct charge. Rabbit, Sheep, Dog, Horse, and Ox all appreciate the Monkey's flexibility and good nature. The Snake will suspect his motives, and these two may wind up trying to out-con each other. The Monkey drives the Tiger to absolute distraction because he can't resist teasing him. Monkeys form immediate mutual admiration societies with other Monkeys—where there is one Monkey, there are usually several.

The Rooster

The Rooster corresponds to the Western sign of Virgo and is ruled by the planet Mercury. Its direction is west and its hours are 5 P.M. to 7 P.M. Summer Roosters are highly verbal and can be critical, whereas winter Roosters tend to be more quietly aggressive, the kind who fix you with an unnerving, glittery stare.

Above all things, Roosters dislike disorganization. They like to administrate everyone and everything around them in the same way that they manage themselves—perfectly. Always precise and efficient, the Rooster born are also critical to a fault, and are never gifted with an overabundance of natural tact. For this reason, they can be quite alienating to others, often unintentionally. While the Rooster can have a downright eccentric exterior, underneath he is likely to be quite traditional. The most combative of all the signs, the Rooster never cowers from the prospect of a good fight, or even a bad one. For better or worse, the Rooster tries to convert everyone to his way of thinking. The Rooster born are fond of the limelight, partly because they believe they deserve it, and partly because they are secretly convinced that they don't.

Excellent organizers and administrators, Roosters have considerable talent for handling other people's money. They live to manage people, schedules, and events. The somewhat bossy nature of the Rooster is tempered, however, by a great sense of humor and fantastic social talents. He genuinely wants the best for everyone, but he may have difficulty in getting what he wants.

Likely to have a highly disciplined mind, the Rooster can be highly intellectual. The workings of the mind are fascinating to them. Since Roosters are perfectionists, they delight in worrying out obscure intellectual problems in a logical, scientific way. And whatever the problem, you can be sure that the solutions of the Rooster will be unique, likely to benefit the whole as well as themselves. They are excellent theoreticians and those annoying little details that can trip up greater minds never pass a Rooster's sharply critical eye unnoticed. Still, the phrase "You can't live with him and you can't live without him" was undoubtedly coined to describe an individual of Rooster proclivities. Interfering and meddlesome, Roosters nevertheless can actually thrive on difficulty and will never desert you in your hour of need, even if you beg them to.

Roosters love to play devil's advocate. They adore arguing and debating the most insignificant point of any problem and are adept at taking any number of stands in an attempt to understand an issue, but diplomatic intricacies are far and away beyond them. A Rooster will start a fight in the street rather than give in to behavior that he considers demeaning or unfair. They are scrappy and independent and although they may be domineering at times, they are usually right—if you can manage to accept their eccentric point of view for a moment. Rooster bravado is often set into operation as a defense mechanism. More than anything, he needs to reassure himself.

Roosters are dramatic and theatrical-looking. They have amazing stamina and like to champion causes (their own and anyone else's) in their streamlined, efficient way. They are practical about complex matters and stumble over the simplest things. They are achievement-oriented, and it is rare to find a Rooster who is an out-and-out failure. Despite the Rooster's practical attitude about money, he is generous with those he loves. He will, however, be adverse to sharing the limelight. Every Rooster is a dependable, reputable worker, though not necessarily a team player. Slothful Roosters are impossible to find. Their great energy and fantastic willpower work to good effect as long as they are well-directed. Roosters never have to range far and wide to make their way in the world—they achieve success and wealth in the most ordinary places and circumstances. Stories of farmers who dug up buried treasure in their own backyard are almost always about Roosters.

Roosters are dreamers destined to succeed at ordinary tasks. Although marvelous self-starters, they need to keep perspective of their grandiosity and sense of self-importance. Don Quixote was undoubtedly a Rooster. Who can say whether or not he could have done with a few less windmills?

Emotions and Relationships

Anyone who wants to truly love a Rooster must first accept his predisposition to controversy. You must understand that there is nothing personal about Rooster fights, even though you will be repeatedly told what is wrong with you and what you must do for "your own good." Roosters are frequently their own worst enemies, particularly in the sphere of personal relationships. The fact that he loves you will not deter him from criticizing the way you talk, dress, or manage your money. Pairing up with a Rooster will almost certainly give you the feeling that you got a lot more than you bargained for. The best you can do about it is to reassure him, anchor his dreams, and make sure he doesn't succumb completely to pervasive delusions of grandeur.

Emotionally, the Rooster is not Mr. Stability. He has frequent and wide-ranging mood swings. When he is happy, he is awe-inspiring; his misery will make you want to jump over a cliff just to get away from it. He is profoundly emotional. Roosters either like or dislike people intensely; indifference is not part of their makeup.

Intimacy is difficult for Roosters because they are naturally independent and see themselves as adventurers. But they are optimists and dauntless friends. "Love Me or Leave Me," is the Rooster's theme song. They are extremely demanding of those who love them, including parents, children, and spouses. Because they must be the center of attention, the home revolves around the Rooster.

Compatibility

The Rooster makes the best match with the wise and intuitive Snake who is cool enough not to overreact to anything the Rooster has to say about him. The Snake appreciates the effervescent personality and dauntless outlook of the Rooster, and the Rooster likes the Snake's quiet understanding. Both highly organized, the Ox and Rooster love keeping to each other's schedules and work together tirelessly. The Dragon appreciates the grandiose plans of the Rooster and may even be able to implement them. Tigers, Sheep, Monkeys, and Boars can all get along quite well with Roosters, as long as all signs remember to give and take.

Rabbits are ill-advised partners because the Rabbit does not understand the Rooster's lack of sensitivity and will be appalled at the scrappy situations into which the Rooster can drag them. Rooster/Rooster relationships are equally stormy. These creatures do everything in their power to battle for the attentions of each other.

The Dog

The sign of the Dog corresponds to the Western sign of Libra. Its planetary ruler is Mercury, and it rules the hours of 7 P.M. to 9 P.M. The direction of the Dog is west-northwest, and Dogs born during the night hours are reputed to be more aggressive and temperamental than those born during the day.

*   *   *

Like its corresponding Western sign of Libra, the sign of the Dog is most distinguished by its sense of justice. The Dog born are loyal, straightforward, and kind, with a sense of fair play that is all but unequaled in the Chinese calendar. Unlike the gentle, peacemaking qualities of the Western sign of Libra, Dogs are vociferous and noisy in righting the world's wrongs.

The Dog has gained a reputation for being one of the more cynical of the signs, but that is not entirely true. Rather, the Dog is simply slower to make friends than some of the more extroverted types, and tends to be suspicious of that which is unfamiliar. Blessed with a powerful, intelligent mind, the Dog nevertheless has very little patience for the subtleties of mixed motives and Hamlet-type dilemmas. In the Dog's-eye view, everything comes down to black and white. Despite what might seem a somewhat simplistic world view, however, the Dog is an astute judge of character, and one of the most loyal of all the signs. No matter what your troubles, the Dog will do everything in his power to end them. Altruistic to a fault, the Dog will frequently put the interests of others before his own.

First impressions count with this sign, and Dog people, whether or not they choose to admit it, are continually categorizing everyone they meet into the good guys and the bad guys, friends and enemies, and serious or trivial personalities. You can rest assured that once the Dog has pronounced his judgment about a person or situation, it will be exceedingly difficult to get him to change his mind. No matter how quick the Dog may be to form conclusions about you, it will take you a long time to get to know him. In many ways, the Dog was born on the defensive. This does not result from feelings of insecurity, but rather from a desire to protect those to whom he feels attached and causes to which he has devoted himself. Because of his suspicious nature, he prefers to get to know others gradually, without a lot of pressure. He may not be as straightforward in expressing himself as he is in his stance on world issues. Get too nosy about the Dog and he is likely to become secretive or altogether withdrawn. Their faithfulness and loyalty can turn to stubbornness and obstinancy and, when challenged or attacked, that friendly, lovable Dog is more than capable of turning vicious and snarling when it comes to protecting his own.

The Dog is a highly verbal sign, and has one of the sharpest tongues in the calendar. Challenge the Dog and prepare yourself for a tongue-lashing of extraordinary clarity, wit, and devastating accuracy. Still, the Dog is never aggressive or combative simply for something to do. This is one personality who chooses his battles very carefully, and his anger is rarely expressed over personal issues. If you manage to rouse the Dog on a more personal level, you can be sure that, uncomfortable as it may be at the time, he will never hold a grudge. The Dog never stays mad for long and never hates forever.

The Dog is not a materialistic sign. Though fond of the creature comforts, he is infinitely more concerned with the problems of the homeless than he is with keeping up with the latest in designer trends. In other words, the Dog is not much given to ceremony or the intricacies of social ritual and has little patience for such pursuits. They do, however, exude an earthy and forthright kind of sex appeal and are bound to attract more than their share of attention. Whereas Horses have a thoroughbred, high-strung sexuality, and Boars are eminently sensual, the Dog is rugged and outdoorsy. They are lively, amiable, and extremely physically appealing, but in an entirely approachable way. These are people others want to touch and respond to in physical demonstrations of affection. Not for the Dog the sexy, veiled mystery of the Snake or even the elegant ease of the Rabbit—what you see is what you get in the Dog's case, and it usually looks pretty good.

Dogs make excellent lawyers, labor leaders, union organizers, and social workers, and can exceed in any public or service-minded profession. Dogs in the arts are devoted to bringing little-known art forms like rhythm and blues into prominence and mass appreciation. Elvis Presley was a Dog native.

Dogs are outraged by injustice and the apparent fraying of the world's moral fibers. They were born to pit their strength against evil, and although they may become increasingly disillusioned and even embittered as time goes on, they are blessed with great reserves of physical strength and moral fortitude. Dogs are the stuff priests, counselors, saints, and martyrs are made of.

Emotions and Relationships

The Dog will always remain independent, but will never stray too far from home. Deeply loyal to those he loves, he is blinded to the faults of others to such an extent that he sticks with them long after the object of their devotion has proved to be completely unworthy. Dogs do not desert their causes easily, but the Dog is rarely overly demonstrative. In fact, they can seem all but immune to the lesser human emotions. Malice, pettiness, and jealousy are beneath Dog dignity, and he is equally unimpressed when these qualities appear in others.

It is not easy for a Dog to trust, but once he does, his heartfelt faith and undivided support brings out the best in those around them. He believes in fair play and, because of this, Dogs are good sports. He is, however, put off by passionate displays and overt declarations. You will not find a Dog giving you flowers and candy, writing you sonnets, or serenading you under your windowsill. He proves his love over time; his commitments are made on a day-to-day basis. He can even be downright alarmed by those who make extravagant gestures. Chances are, his suspicious nature will convince him that such extravagance would not be necessary, unless you had something to hide.

Once won, the love of the Dog will suffer untold amounts of abuse before the Dog deserts the object of his affections. And even at that, he is likely to carry the torch for a long time to come.

Compatibility

Horses and Tigers provide excellent Dog partners. All share the qualities of forthrightness and loyalty. Rats, Snakes, Monkeys, Boars, and other Dogs provide companionship and should experience little in the way of conflict. Dog/Rooster combinations are difficult. Roosters are entirely too critical of the idealistic Dog's worldview, and the Dog does not understand why the Rooster has to be so everlastingly theatrical and grandiose. Dogs and Dragons are unfortunate; the Dragon is entirely too overblown and confident for the Dog. Dogs rarely find happiness with moody, self-indulgent Sheep, and the Sheep finds the Dog upsetting and critical. Somewhat surprisingly, Dogs and Rabbits make lifelong friends and lovers. The Rabbit admires the Dog's steadfastness and helps to ease the Dog's diplomatic relationships with the world at large.

The Boar

The Boar corresponds to the Western sign of Scorpio, ruled by Saturn. The hours ruled by the Boar are 9 P.M. to 11 P.M. Its direction is north-northwest. Boars born during the summer are more prone to excess of all kinds than are those born during the winter months.

* * *

Nice guys finish last, and the Chinese calendar ends with the sign of the Boar. Honest, simple, and sturdy, the Boar is one of the most natural, easygoing personalities around. They are popular, well-liked, and have a cheerful outlook and earthy sense of humor. Like the Sheep and Rabbit, the Boar seeks harmony above all else. These people let bygones be bygones and never hold a grudge. The Boar is a great believer in giving people enough rope to hang themselves. Sociable and good-humored, the Boar is a naturally happy, well-adjusted sign. Boars love parties, clubs, and celebrations of all kinds. They were born for extended networks and associations. Incapable of deception themselves, Boars do not understand it in others and would rather be led to the slaughter than live in an intrigue of lies. They are sincere, warm-hearted, and trustworthy. Often they have difficulty in understanding other, more devious types, so it is easy to pull the wool over a Boar's eyes. Boars are perennially innocent and can be quite sincerely confused by the Machiavellian machinations of other, more crafty animal signs.

The Boar is the original soft touch and will open his home and give out money to all. He is generous to those he loves and those he wants to love him, and will share everything he has, even to his own detriment. Chances are the Boar will go bankrupt at least once in his life, but he will take full responsibility and will never be down for long. Boar people often allow others to take advantage of them, but the Boar is never without resources.

He has a genius for attracting money and help from others, and his resoluteness, cheerful attitude, and resilience are sure to see him through even the most trying of circumstances.

Ingenuous though the Boar may appear, he is never stupid. Boars live by the code that "what is yours will come to you," and the Boar is not averse to waiting a long time for that to happen. He sustains a great inner belief in the rhythm of nature and the sensuality of life. This is perhaps the secret to his strength. Boars work hard, but do so with grace and gentleness. These are people who make work look easy; suffering is not part of their style. Although they are sensitive souls, they can dismiss criticism and conflict with a shrug and are strong enough to sustain great misfortune without undue damage to their finer qualities. Because of his innate generosity, the Boar is considered fortunate indeed, and will rarely have to face the destructive ups and downs of the Tiger, Dragon, or Horse. His resilience, fortitude, and generally scrupulous character will carry him through.

Though highly intelligent, the Boar is not terribly deep. Their philosophic approach to life can border on the superstitious and fatalistic. If they are pushed up against a wall, feeling as though they have nothing left to lose, they can go on bouts of self-gratification and self-destruction that would make Henry the Eighth look like an ascetic.

Above all, Boars love the good things in life. They have enormous physical appetites and, without self-control, can be exploited and debased in all kinds of debauchery. Boars can, however, work as hard as they play. Their basic talents, conscientiously applied, insure triumphs. And triumphant, the Boar will provide for any and all the members of his entourage. The neighbor who routinely barbecues rib-eye steaks for everyone living in a ten-block radius is undoubtedly a Boar.

Boars excel in business, social work, and charity and are among the best fund-raisers around. They seek practical solutions to problems and can get others enthusiastic about causes, simply because they know the Boar not only believes what he's saying, but has also given a fair amount of money of his own. They are superb chefs and lovers. They are excellent at managing people and make understanding and sympathetic personnel managers. Their innate appreciation of the arts makes them superb patrons, philanthropists, and producers.

Emotions and Relationships

Boar hearts are permanently affixed to their sleeves. Warm-hearted and honest, it is impossible for any Boar to hide emotions. Sexy and sensual, the physical side of love is never far from the Boar's thoughts. He would rather express his love physically than intellectually, but his tempestuous affairs generally end with the Boar as the injured party. Still, Boars were born for commitment and their hearts never stay broken for too long.

The phrase "ask and you shall receive" describes the Boar perfectly, but he is nevertheless scrupulous to a fault. His fabled generosity requires that the Boar be on the giving rather than the receiving end of things, and he is most happy when he is most magnanimous. Besides, it can be unwise to overindulge the already indulgent Boar. The Boar will give you anything you ask, but territorial types beware. Boars will just as happily help themselves to anything in your closet, your refrigerator, or your liquor cabinet.

No one can love with such abandonment as the Boar, and yet he prefers to keep his sentiments secret and even anonymous. He worships from afar for years and years without the loved one's having the slightest inkling of his feelings, and he manages to take care of his physical needs in more practical ways. It is likely that the Boar has developed the ability to keep his head and body separate. He loves with all his heart, but if that love is not appropriate or adequately reciprocated, you can be sure that the rest of his body will remain happily occupied elsewhere.

If he has complaints, you can be sure that he will express himself in mild, jovial ways. He takes sincere criticism well and will genuinely try to do better if his faults are pointed out. In his generosity he may tend to do too much, overdo his devotion and smother those he loves, which will not go over well with independent types. Boars are close to their parents and anyone else who approves of them. As parents themselves, they generally spoil their children.

Quick-tempered himself, the Boar hates fighting and always ends by giving the other person the benefit of the doubt. They respond well to reason or food in states of emotional excess. If you are in the wrong, chances are the Boar won't be the one to tell you so. Boars are strong, tough customers with powerful backs to carry what problems come to them, those they love, and even complete strangers. They are sympathetic listeners and practical helpers. Boars value security and, at the same time, they take it for granted.

Compatibility

Boars are happiest with the gentle Sheep or the elegant Rabbit. The Sheep understands the Boar tendency to self-indulge. The Rabbit refines the rougher aspects of the Boar's character. Boars can also get along well with Tigers and their antics. Boar/Boar relationships often don't have enough spark to keep either party interested for long. Rats, Oxen, Dragons, Horses, Roosters, and Dogs prove favorable because the Boar is easygoing and tolerant of their more rambunctious ways. Boars have great difficulty with Monkeys and Snakes. Both signs are too complex, cunning, and wily for the Boar.

Listed here are the years of each animal sign from 1900 to the year 2000. Note that because the Chinese calendar operates according to a lunar system, the starting and ending dates for each *lunar* year do change.

TABLE 1-1—THE ANIMAL SIGNS

THE YEARS OF THE RAT:
January 31, 1900 to February 18, 1901
February 16, 1912 to February 5, 1913
February 5, 1924 to January 24, 1925
January 24, 1936 to February 10, 1937
February 10, 1948 to January 28, 1949
January 28, 1960 to February 14, 1961
January 16, 1972 to February 2, 1973
February 2, 1984 to February 19, 1985
February 19, 1996 to February 7, 1997

THE YEARS OF THE OX:
February 19, 1901 to February 7, 1902
February 6, 1913 to January 25, 1914
January 25, 1925 to February 12, 1926
February 11, 1937 to January 30, 1938
January 29, 1949 to February 16, 1950
February 16, 1961 to February 4, 1962
February 3, 1973 to January 22, 1974
February 20, 1985 to February 8, 1986
February 8, 1997, to January 27, 1998

THE YEARS OF THE TIGER:
February 8, 1902 to January 28, 1903
January 26, 1914 to February 13, 1915
February 13, 1926 to February 1, 1927
January 31, 1938 to February 18, 1939
February 17, 1950 to February 5, 1951
February 5, 1962 to January 24, 1963
January 23, 1974 to February 10, 1975
February 9, 1986 to January 28, 1987
January 28, 1997 to February 5, 1999

THE YEARS OF THE RABBIT:
January 29, 1903 to February 15, 1904
February 14, 1915 to February 2, 1916
February 2, 1927 to January 22, 1928
February 19, 1939 to February 7, 1940
February 6, 1951 to January 26, 1952
January 25, 1963 to February 12, 1964
February 11, 1975 to January 30, 1976
January 29, 1987 to February 16, 1988
February 6, 1999 to January 27, 2000

THE YEARS OF THE DRAGON:
February 16, 1904 to February 3, 1905
February 3, 1916 to January 22, 1917
January 23, 1928 to February 9, 1929
February 8, 1940 to January 26, 1941
January 27, 1952 to February 13, 1953
February 13, 1964 to February 1, 1965
January 31, 1976 to February 17, 1977
February 17, 1988 to February 5, 1989

THE YEARS OF THE SNAKE
February 4, 1905 to January 24, 1906
January 23, 1917 to February 10, 1918
February 10, 1929 to January 29, 1930
January 27, 1941 to February 14, 1942
February 14, 1953 to February 2, 1954
February 2, 1965 to January 20, 1966
February 18, 1977 to February 6, 1978
February 6, 1989 to January 26, 1990

THE YEARS OF THE HORSE
January 25, 1906 to February 12, 1907
February 11, 1918 to January 31, 1919

January 30, 1930 to February 16, 1931
February 15, 1942 to February 4, 1943
February 3, 1954 to January 23, 1955
January 21, 1966 to February 8, 1967
February 7, 1978 to January 27, 1979
January 27, 1990 to February 14, 1991

THE YEARS OF THE SHEEP

February 13, 1907 to February 1, 1908
February 1, 1919 to February 20, 1920
February 17, 1931 to February 5, 1932
February 5, 1943 to January 24, 1944
January 24, 1955 to February 11, 1956
February 9, 1967 to January 29, 1968
January 28, 1979 to February 15, 1980
February 15, 1991 to February 3, 1992

THE YEARS OF THE MONKEY

February 2, 1908 to January 21, 1909
February 20, 1920 to February 7, 1921
February 6, 1932 to January 25, 1933
January 25, 1944 to February 12, 1945
February 12, 1956 to January 30, 1957
January 30, 1968 to February 16, 1969
February 16, 1980, to February 4, 1981
February 4, 1992 to January 22, 1993

THE YEARS OF THE ROOSTER

January 22, 1909 to February 9, 1910
February 8, 1921 to January 27, 1922
January 26, 1933 to February 13, 1934
February 13, 1945 to February 1, 1946
January 31, 1957 to February 17, 1958

February 17, 1969 to February 5, 1970
February 5, 1981, to January 24, 1982
January 23, 1993 to February 9, 1994

THE YEARS OF THE DOG
February 10, 1910 to January 29, 1911
January 28, 1922 to February 15, 1923
February 14, 1934 to February 3, 1935
February 2, 1946 to January 21, 1947
February 18, 1958 to February 7, 1959
February 6, 1970 to January 26, 1971
January 25, 1982 to February 12, 1983
February 10, 1994 to January 30, 1995

THE YEARS OF THE BOAR
January 30, 1911 to February 17, 1912
February 16, 1923 to February 4, 1924
February 4, 1935 to January 23, 1936
January 22, 1947 to February 9, 1948
February 8, 1959 to January 27, 1960
January 27, 1971 to January 15, 1972
February 13, 1983 to February 1 1984
January 31, 1995 to February 18, 1996.

Chapter Two

THE ELEMENTS

Chinese astrology, healing practices, martial arts, and philosophy are all intimately related to the theory of the Five Elements or Five Forces. The Five Forces are Water, Fire, Wood, Metal, and Earth, and they are thought to be the five ways in which energy expresses itself in the natural world.

If this sounds complicated and suspiciously esoteric to you, stop for a second and remember a game that you played when you were a child. The game was called Scissors, Paper, and Rock. The players stood or sat in a circle. At the count of three, each player displayed one of five hand positions. A closed fist meant rock, an open-palm designated paper, a fist with the thumb up was dynamite, two index fingers separated from a closed fist stood for scissors, and no hand signal at all meant water.

The point of the game was that each "element" interacted with other elements: paper wrapped rock, rock crushed scissors, scissors cut paper, dynamite blew up scissors, water soaked dynamite, and on and on in an endless cycle. The player who chose the dominant element of the game had the satisfaction of licking his fingers and whacking the wrist of the player or players who had chosen the losing elements of any given round. The more enthusiastic players often raised welts. But sooner or later, and often in the same round of the game, everyone got whacked.

This simple children's game taught us all—even if we didn't know what we were learning at the time—that there were five elements in the world, and that all were interchangeably powerful and weak. It isn't hard to figure out that dynamite stood for fire; scissors for metal; rock for earth; paper for wood; water for water.

All energy (known as *ch'i* to the Chinese) was described by ancient Chinese philosophers as being broken down into one of these five ways of manifesting energy in the natural world. The essence of these properties, it was believed, identified and characterized all matter. After first identifying these forces, the Chinese went on to associate the elements with natural rhythms, seasons, weather, landscapes, home interiors, the human body, fighting styles, art, human personality, colors, planets, tastes, and sensations. Each energy form was constantly in process and in motion in the universe.

In the natural creative cycle, Metal holds and creates Water, Water nurtures Wood, Wood feeds Fire, Fire produces Earth through its ashes, and Earth creates Metal. In the natural destructive cycle, Metal chops Wood, Wood depletes the Earth, Earth obstructs Water, Water puts out Fire, and Fire melts Metal.

This elemental energy theory existed long before Buddhism made inroads into China. It is said to have been created by the Yellow Emperor Huang Ti, first of three prehistoric Chinese emperors, who began his reign in 2266 B.C. and who is credited with the invention of agriculture and farming, bricks, musical instruments, and much of what constitutes the roots of modern Chinese philosophy. It is said that his wife domesticated the first silkworms. The hexagram of Huang Ti means father, yellow, son, and grandson. He is considered by the Chinese to be the father of their people, no small accomplishment in a country whose belief system holds that the world was created by immortals. Huang Ti was the first emperor who was completely human, who had no divine blood.

Huang Ti is perhaps best remembered for his considerable philosophical abilities. It is he, and later Lao-Tsu, who laid the foundations for Taoism. The Taoism of Huang Ti and Lao-Tsu was quite different from Taoism as we know it today, which has since been greatly influenced by Buddhism, introduced to China in the first century. Before the advent of Buddhism into Chinese thought, Taoism existed as an alternative philosophical path to the Confucian system. Early Taoists concerned themselves with the metaphysical. Confucianism offered a moralistic solution to the ills of the world.

Simply put, Confucianism was a religion that concentrated on man in society and his dutiful interaction with nature and other men. It was only after the influence of Buddhism on Chinese thought that Taoism graduated from the realms of philosophy to the status of a full-fledged religion, complete with monasteries, nunneries, rituals, and liturgy.

The Chinese hold the Three Teachings—Confucianism, Taoism, and Buddhism—in great regard and consider each to lead to knowledge of the infinite if approached correctly. According to Chinese tradition, the "correct approach" is through inquiry—questions and answers, the process of making choices—essentially a Socratic method. Inquiry was considered to form the basis of the teaching and learning of these philosophies. Students found or were assigned a master whose job it was to lead them through the system of choice.

Taoism held that all living things, the universe and the individual, came into existence and moved as a result of forces of energy. Human beings conduct *ch'i*, an energy force, through the body. An imbalance in this vital force was believed to cause all manner of irregularities: illness, personality disorders, and psychological dysfunction. By rebalancing the flow of energy through the body, human beings could allow the body to heal itself. The energy force that operated in the world at large was called the *Tao*, a word meaning the natural ways and processes of all living things. If one's environment was balanced and in accord with the laws of nature, one could not help but act in a meaningful way. As *ch'i* operates in the human body, so the Great Tao operates in the universe.

Although this seems like an abstract, lofty premise on which to base a world view, the Chinese used the principle of the Tao to create a sophisticated, workable medical system based on energy meridians, herbalism, and balanced amounts of rest and activity, which is still being explored by medical practitioners today. Taoists developed methods of breath control and exercises originally designed to promote longevity, which eventually developed into a stunningly effective system of martial arts. All of these social contributions used as their basis the concept of the movement of energy through the body according to five principal energy "styles"—the Five Elements.

The Elements and the Horoscope

The Chinese belief in the Five Forces naturally extends to the system of astrology. The ways in which these elements affect the individual chart can be either very obvious or very subtle, simple or complex, and will be discussed at greater length in subsequent chapters. In Chinese astrology, each element manifests itself first in its positive or active aspect, then in its negative or receptive side. For example, the year of the positive earth dragon is always followed by the year of the negative earth snake. Because there are five elements, each with two aspects, the elemental cycle completes itself every ten years, at which time it repeats itself. How the ten-year elemental cycle complements and coincides with the twelve-year animal sign cycle will also be discussed in detail later on. First, it is best to familiarize yourself with the nature of the elements as perceived by the Chinese, in order to gain a better understanding of how they can be applied to this system of astrology.

To determine what elements are dominant in your chart, refer to the tables at the end of this chapter. Keep in mind that there are five elemental influences in any chart: the Animal sign, the year, the hour, the date, and the country of birth will all have elemental associations. Ideally, all elements will be represented. Most people, however, have a predominance of one or two elements.

Metal

In the Oriental view, Metal at its best and most positive is represented by gold. At its worst, it can be represented as a sword. Think of it this way— money, or gold, represents prosperity and interaction between people. At its worst, the sword, it can turn terrible and destructive. Metal corresponds to the color white, the autumn of the year, and dry, cool weather.

Metal energy is seen as being able to do the following things: hold and support structures, contain emotions, conduct electricity, either in a real or metaphorical sense, and relay information. Metal can inspire and communicate, or it can incite and destroy. Metal is the energy responsible for people coming together in a common, objective cause, or it can turn those same people against one another. Metal is the element of information. It is the power of intuition expressed in practical, useful ways.

In the human body, the element of Metal rules the lungs. It is interesting to note that Metal-dominated personalities frequently have respiratory trouble. Its sensory organ is the nose and its secondary organ is the large intestine.

Metal emotions can be seen as autumnal. Romantic and sometimes sad, Metal energy is associated with longing, wistfulness, and even homesickness. Positive Metal emotions are righteousness and a highly developed sense of right, wrong, and justice.

The Metal Personality

As rigid and resolute as the individual Animal signs will permit, the Metal personality is guided by strong feelings and will pursue objectives with astonishing singlemindedness and little hesitation. Metal influence in a chart imparts strength, communicative powers, and boundless ambition.

The Metal person usually has a strong sense of self and the will and determination to succeed in almost any undertaking. This type has a great ability to bring others together in all sorts of interactions, but he himself is usually a loner and may be solitary minded to a fault—the kind of person whose innate sense of independence causes him to withdraw and even refuse the help and support of those who offer it. When it comes to the finer aspects of human relationships, the Metal personality can be his own worst enemy.

It can be said of Metal people that they are stubborn and inflexible, though to be fair, their refusal to be swayed from any given path, opinion, or course of action is usually guided by an inner conviction. These people have a kind of unshakable faith in themselves and their own abilities, and any challenge to that vision is likely only to strengthen their resolve. When the Metal person has decided to play one of his hunches, almost nothing on heaven or on earth will succeed in convincing him that that hunch is erroneous. They can be stubborn, unadaptable, and even unreasonable, but to give credit where credit it due, Metal people are almost always proven to be right in the end. This is one case where what looks like megalomania is actually ambition guided by self-knowledge.

The Metal-minded are never flighty. They take themselves seriously and that serious attitude makes them capable of prolonged and patient effort. Failure and distraction make little impression on them. If they do encounter problems, however, Metal people like to solve them alone. A Metal person in difficulty is not someone you'll see a great deal of. He won't call you up to cry on your shoulder or talk things out. It's almost as if they find it necessary to shun the help and solicitations of others in order to go inward and draw on those deep reserves of intuition before they can even begin to make the necessary adjustments.

Physically, Metal people tend to be very strong-looking and a great deal of Metal in a chart is thought to be a sign of longevity. They have strong impulses, great generative and regenerative powers, and are at their best when bringing their powers for change and transformation into play. Blessed with a highly developed olfactory sense, the Metal person responds favorably to bouquets of flowers around the house just as he responds unfavorably to unpleasant odors. If you have a date with a Metal person, be sure to dab on a little extra fragrance. It is sure to make an impression.

Self-made types, Metal people possess great financial and accumulative instincts, and more often than not will use them to support their highly developed sense of independence. Millionaires, moguls, and entrepreneurs, they can also excel in any profession where they can inspire others to a common goal. Their highly developed sense of justice makes them great statesmen and champions of the downtrodden. Winston Churchill was Metal dominated.

Metal people can be prone to bouts of almost unendurable sadness, which they relate to the conditions surrounding them in their environment. These are people who are driven to pace the street in order to work out their problems, only to find their sensitive natures further saddened by urban decay, homelessness, and the injustice of life. Their streaks of melancholia can help them to be empathetic to others in trouble, but sometimes the Metal person may find life just too much to bear.

Difficult and sometimes downright ornery, the Metal personality is nevertheless almost always exciting and interesting to be around. They possess a rare combination of real intellect and genuine intuition, and if they can learn to control their inflexibility and need to make others conform to their way of thinking, they can prove to be the best and most loyal of friends and associates.

Given the profile, the Metal person's task is clear. They must learn to temper their single-mindedness with flexibility, their strong opinions with a willingness to listen and allow differences, and augment their solitary streak with strong social influences. It is important for the Metal person to laugh at himself occasionally and not cut himself off from others just because they may not take him as seriously as he does himself.

Water

In the creative cycle of the five elements, Metal gives us Water. Think of a tin cup filled with water and the condensation that forms on the outside; just as the container holds water it can also be said to produce it. Conversely, Metal turns to liquid when heated. The Water element is most closely related to the arts and the expression of the inner being. The active expression of Water in nature is a wave, but Water can be passively expressed as a stagnant pond. Soft rainfall nurtures the earth and growing things, but hurricanes are destructive forces that wreak havoc on everything they touch. Water corresponds to the color blue, the season of winter and cold, wet weather.

The energy of Water can reflect with clarity and beauty the things that are around it. Water indirectly influences whatever it comes into contact with and can nourish the living or wear down the strongest stone. Water communicates emotionally, with sensitivity and understanding, and helps people to relate to each other on an empathetic level. Water cannot stand and fight for its cause. Rather, it can wear away, penetrate, and evaporate conflict and resistance. The element of Water is a great enabler; it can help people to understand each other and to solve problems through emotional methods rather than logical ones.

In the human body, Water rules the kidneys and is secondarily associated with the ear and the bladder. Water-dominated people often have extraordinary hearing. If they are not musically gifted, they will almost surely appreciate it. Emotionally, Water is associated with fear, stress, and nervousness. Because of their hypersensitivity to people and situations around them, Water people often incorporate others' fears along with their own, and they can feel immense stress when physically overloaded. Positively, Water is emotionally associated with gentleness, sympathy, and caring. Water people are kind and go out of their way to help those in need.

The Water Personality

Water people have a better than average ability to communicate. They are not straightforward and are never blunt, preferring a gentler, more diplomatic approach to getting their ideas across. Water types subtly and pervasively influence the thoughts of others through emotional interaction and closeness. And they can listen as well as they can talk. Their talent for communication exists on more than one level though, and most are psychically gifted to some degree. All Water people are sensitive to the vibrations around them. Verbal or nonverbal, visible or invisible, the Water person somehow takes it all in. Water types make excellent negotiators and have an almost magical ability to know how, when, or whom to approach at any given time in order to advance their beliefs or solve their problems. They can, however, be walking human sponges, picking up impressions and hunches at random to such an extent that they simply lose track of their objectives and goals. They must, on occasion, desensitize themselves to their surroundings or run the risk of simply being overcome by the world around them.

This personality is flexible to a fault and can be too adaptable to life around him. Nevertheless, they have an unerring, and generally very charming, ability to make others want what they want, often inspiring those same people to go out and get it for them. Exhausting personal confrontation, warriorlike battles with the world, and scrapping their way up the ladder of success are not part of the Water style.

A predominately Water person would invariably rather infiltrate than dominate. Where the Metal personality will play a hunch and back lost causes until Armageddon, the Water person uses his intuition in more pervasive and insidious ways. Like a wave, this personality gently persuades and retreats, convinces and disappears with unremitting regularity until his case is finally won. You may think a disagreement with a Water person is over when he changes the subject, but rest assured it is not. He is certain to make the same, quiet, gentle argument, present the same set of pleas, and bring a nearly identical tear to his eye the next time you see him. They can wear down and, yes, even whine until they get what they want, but if you do harbor a certain suspicion that you're being manipulated, it is rare to feel any real antagonism about it because the Water person is inevitably winsome and charming in his demands.

The Water viewpoint is rarely narrow or restricted. These people are highly aware and, perhaps because they are so capable of seeing the whole picture, can be relied upon to predict future trends with great accuracy. Like their element, they are fluid. Graceful in body and human relations, they move easily through all sorts of circumstances, social contacts, and life situations. The often unobtrusive Water personality usually has a great deal of life experience under his belt, much of which is not necessarily evident behind his soft-spoken, gentle, and even passive exterior. At their worst, a Water person can be something of a pushover, entirely too conciliatory and liable to take the path of least resistance or disappear altogether. They can give the appearance of being quite fickle or changeable at times and too dependent upon others for their support. It may be difficult for some more forthright types ever to entirely trust the Water person—you may find yourself crying on his shoulder and pouring out your life secrets to him, only to discover him next week at a neighboring bar being just as sympathetic to someone he has met two minutes ago! One may wonder whether these people live on the emotions of others or whether they really do care. The Water person does care, but that doesn't necessarily mean that he considers sympathy and intimacy the same thing. Think about it—when was the last time that Water type poured out his heart to you?

Basically, the Water person identifies so strongly with the person or people that surround him that he is quite capable of running through emotions the way other people do paperclips. It is not that they lack emotion, but rather that they understand it too well. The Water person realizes that emotions change, sometimes from moment to moment. Hearts change, injuries change, minds change—and the Water person changes right along with them.

You might also suspect him of using you and somehow magically filling up your mind with his ideas in order to get his way. Be assured that the Water person is only doing what he thinks is best for you and, because of his highly intuitive nature, he is generally right. He rarely has a grand design of his own, even though his influence may go in all directions. Rather, he feels his way through life and can play out its discordant themes beautifully.

Water people are prone to nervous disorders and breakdowns, yet their great resilience enables them to pull through. They react strongly to the emotions of others and recuperate amazingly well if they can learn to keep away from negative influences and nurture themselves. These people rarely spend any time by themselves. Their fears arise more from being overextended than self-absorbed; no matter how bad their state, you can always depend on a Water person to be out and about. They have an amazing ability to survive that runs completely contrary to their often fragile exteriors. These are people who depend on the kindness of strangers and generally get it. They trust the universe implicitly until they are badly hurt by it. They can absorb a friend's bad mood or a sudden drop in barometric pressure with equal intensity and, worse, somehow manage to internalize it. They can be hypersensitive and over-imaginative and, at their very worst, paranoid. Almost all Water people are artistically inclined in some way, although they may have difficulty in concentrating their interests in one discipline. Perhaps Mary Pickford is one of the best examples of the Water-dominated personality. She was America's Sweetheart, invented with gentle, fragile goodness and fantastic emotional appeal by an adoring public. Yet, while America was watching her at the movies, she was quietly using that same big-eyed influence to form real estate conglomerates that would wind up owning half of Hollywood—making her one of the richest women in the world. Such is the mind of the Water dominated.

Wood

Wood energy is created by water. Without the nourishment of Water, Wood could not come into being. Wood energy can express itself in the character of the strongest oak or flexible, pliant bamboo. Fortunately aspected, Wood energy can form the staff that enables you to climb the steepest paths. Poorly expressed, it can be as primitive and dangerous as a pointed spear. The element of Wood corresponds to the color green, the season of spring, and warm, moist weather.

In the human body, the Wood element rules the liver. Its sensory organs are the eyes, and its secondary organ is the gallbladder. Emotionally, Wood is associated with anger and kindness.

In nature, Wood energy is responsible for the growth and renewal of all living things. If you think of a tree, you will see it is a system of organic administration. The roots secure the tree to the earth and draw water and nourishment from the soil, the trunk supports it, the branches spread out, and the leaves that cover the branches draw nourishment from the sun for the entire structure. All parts are essential to the good of the whole. Wood energy expands, develops, shelters, and makes resources readily available to others. It has a strong sense of community. The tree sees the interrelatedness of life, the interdependence of all life systems.

The Wood Personality

The Wood-dominated personality has an expansive, cooperative nature that allows him to do things on a grand scale. Wood people are marked by executive ability; their managerial instincts enable them to delegate responsibility and convince others to join forces with them. They have an almost magical ability to turn finances, information, and ideas into profitable enterprises of all kinds. Because they inspire trust, people come to their aid with financial, emotional, and personal support. It is rare to find a Wood person in solitary pursuit of his objectives or pleasures. These people are highly social; they invariably have a wide range of acquaintances and resources to draw upon. They are extroverts who thrive on the complexities of human interaction, although not necessarily in personal ways. They are experts at problem solving and being able to pinpoint where an individual can best contribute to an organization or group effort of any kind.

They are detail-oriented and believe that there are few problems, especially in business, that cannot be remedied by expansion. They are incredibly energetic. For example, the Wood-dominated woman is the kind who will have absolutely no problem with the intricacies of running a corporation and being a wife and mother. What may seem like overwhelming responsibility to others will be completely natural to the Wood person.

The Wood personality is always liable to have one foot in the future. They see the long view and constantly have some sort of long-range plan in the works. However, they are not intuitive visionaries like the Metal-dominated. The Wood-dominated plan is almost always very practical.

Of all the elements, the Wood person is perhaps the most ethical, and these people expect the same high moral standards from others. There is no tolerance here for those who are deceptive or double dealing. Equally impatient with actual as well as moral laziness, they demonstrate no understanding whatever for those who pad their expense accounts, take long lunches, or fail to pull their own weight. There is little insecurity in the Wood personality. They have egos that can be as big as their plans. This element takes his own part in things as seriously as he does everyone else's and expects his due in respect and appreciation for that part. They are rarely self-effacing.

The Wood person does not deal well in abstraction; his goals are practical and workable. He may not be able to discern future trends intuitively the way a Water person can but, given the facts, he is usually able to turn his information into a profit. Fast-food franchises were almost certainly the brainchild of a Wood personality.

Wood people are highly visual and always have an eye out for detail. They are the kind who undoubtedly walk into a room and straighten that picture on the wall, but they are so charming and social that you're unlikely to be offended by the intrusion. If the Wood person is artistically inclined, it is likely to be in the area of the visual arts rather than something less tangible. If involved in creative pursuits, they prefer, quite literally, to be able to "see" the results.

The Wood dominated have to curb their tempers. They are subject to all kinds of frustration, due to the simple fact that not all things can be depended upon to operate according to the Wood person's highly organized vision. Badly aspected, Wood energy can scatter itself, starting huge projects and not finishing them, or spreading itself too thin in an attempt to find the perfect climate for growth. Also, the Wood personality is often impatient. They may try to force certain outcomes and dissipate their energies in frustration when things do not happen on schedule. When Wood people are in need of renewal and recharging of their energies, the best place for them is in art galleries, museums or, best of all, out in nature.

As good as Wood people may be at understanding and motivating others, they sometimes find it very difficult to express themselves. Although they may have a wide range of associates, they are likely to have few close friends. As capable as they are at grand designs and brilliant organizations, they often feel less than adequate when it comes to the specific give-and-take of one on one. It may take a long time to truly get to know the Wood personality.

They are terrific people to work for because they are kind and compassionate to everyone; they are sure to share the glory. The quintessential team player, the Wood person believes that the achievements of the whole reflect well on him. And the Wood person is always entirely too ethical to go around stealing another's thunder. Physically active, the Wood person performs equally well at team sports.

The Wood-dominated person must be careful to develop a greater understanding of personal freedom without always feeling compelled to sacrifice individuality (their own and everyone else's) to the larger vision. They must make themselves more accessible in the realm of personal relationships and not give in to anger and frustration when things don't go precisely according to plan. If they can tolerate the Water personality's seeming lack of focus, they can learn a lot from such types. Above all, patience should be the watchword here. Their natural kindness and practicality will do the rest.

Fire

In the natural cycle, wood fuels fire. Fire could not exist without it, and fires can be started by rubbing two sticks together. Fire corresponds to the color red, the season of summer and hot, dry weather. It rules the heart. Its sensory organ is the tongue and its secondary organ is the small intestine.

Fire can warm, comfort, and cheer; it can also burn and destroy. In nature, Fire energy expresses itself by bringing light to the world or by bringing about violent changes like explosions, conflagrations, and eruptions. Fire can be a civilizing factor—consider how primitive man changed when he first began to cook his food, how tribes gathered and began to communicate around the element of Fire. Fire illuminates injustice and inspires action. Badly aspected, the element of Fire can express itself in mindless passion, bloody revolution, mob rule, or the cruelty of an Inquisition—a force of nature that lays waste to all without discrimination. Emotionally the element of Fire is associated with cruelty and impatience, but it is also associated with honor, respect, and love.

The Fire Personality

The Fire-dominated personality is a great natural leader. They are movers and shakers, people who can inspire others on to great deeds. They are charismatic and sometimes dangerously driven. Everyone is attracted to the warmth and emotional passion of the Fire personality. These people have a sixth sense when it comes to being where the action is. If there is no action to be found, the Fire person is sure to spark something of interest before long, but that same small spark can easily turn into anything from the pleasant joys of the hearth to a towering inferno. Either way, the result is sure to attract the attention of large crowds in the shortest possible period of time. The Fire person believes that problems should be solved with action—any action. They love new things, new ideas, and change of almost any kind. And yet, for all their love of the new, they are rarely farsighted. They often fail to consider the consequences of their actions and are most likely to leap before they look, usually taking a number of followers along with them! The Fire personality has almost no sense of danger or of self preservation.

Because of his radical outlook and headstrong lifestyle, the Fire person is fated to encounter lots of ups and downs in life. Fire people can inspire passionate involvement and loyalty, but these things are likely to be short-lived, simply because the Fire dominated can catapult their associates into difficulties with little regard for the outcome. Fire people love to be center stage and are quite capable of exploiting others for their own ends. They make great speech makers, not great listeners; great orators but poor humanitarians.

Yet the Fire person is dynamic, exciting, and unhampered by the rules and regulations that sometimes govern fainter hearts. Given the right set of circumstances they can, like Daniel Webster, actually beat the devil on occasion. The fire person is never duplicitous; you always know exactly where they stand. They make decisions quicky and easily and are never at a loss for words. They can be exhausting, but they are never treacherous. Fire people make great creators and inventors and can bring even the most obscure theories and ideas into actuality faster than any other elemental type. They have almost no notion of failure or defeat. They charge ahead optimistically, sure that they can match any opponent, overcoming any obstacle in their way. They are invariably brave; they make the best soldiers, warriors, and mercenaries, although not necessarily the best generals.

Fire people have been responsible for sweeping social changes, and if in retrospect the price of those changes seems high, at least they were accomplished. If the ends do not entirely justify the means, well, those are points for scholars and historians to debate, not Fire personalities. The French Revolution is a fine example of Fire power at work, but then, so is Joan of Arc.

Fire people are passionate in everything they do. They can be of enormous benefit to others and are always intense, if somewhat demanding. The Fire personality is marked by a sarcastic wit and often brilliant sense of humor. They are capable of an extraordinary capacity for love. This is the element that gave rise to things like opera and skywritten proposals of marriage. They bring a sense of drama to ordinary lives and events, and we are frequently left the better, if a little breathless, for their influence. The Fire personality's tempestuousness is almost always packaged with flair and charm and they have a charismatic look to them that is hard to beat, much less ignore. Take a quick inventory of the local avant-garde, and you're sure to discover a Fire personality or two.

They are ambitous, but not competitive. The grubby struggle up the corporate ladder is not for the Fire type; he or she is more likely to topple the ladder and leap the wall in a single bound, leaving more ordinary mortals to gape in admiration and, in a word, eat the dust.

Clearly, the Fire-dominated personality needs to temper his natural enthusiasm with a little patience and quite a bit in the way of discrimination. If he cannot find those qualities within, then he should, as the saying goes, "let cooler heads prevail."

Earth

Fire, once it has burned away the dross, returns wood to the earth in the form of its ashes. Earth, following the cycle of fire, is calming, peaceful, and regenerative. Earth people have astonishing powers of creating things surely and methodically. At its best, Earth is the summation of all things and provides the stability out of which all things obtain growth and life. At worst, it is smothering and confining, capable of burying the more mutable personalities. Earth corresponds to the life-giving color yellow. Its season is Indian summer and it resonates to mild weather. In the human body, Earth rules the spleen and pancreas. Its sense organ is the mouth and its secondary organ is the stomach.

The energy of the Earth is seen as patient, rhythmic, and enduring. Earth people are built to last. Earth energy can move easily between the cycles of the seasons and paces the energy of other personalities to the more eternal rhythms of birth, death, and rebirth. Earth energy carries ancient knowledge that comes from its ability to transform reality in primal, instinctual ways. Earth resonates to the other energies; it can ground the inherent electricity of the Metal element, nourish itself with Water, aborb the ashes of Fire, and both absorb Wood and cause its birth.

The energy of the Earth is said to possess the quality of fairness, based on this element's singular ability to weigh the pros and cons of any issue against that which is truly important in the world. Negatively, Earth energy gone haywire can cause Earth-dominated personalities to become eternal worriers—people who never rest and who are forever trying to anticipate problems even before they arise.

The Earth Personality

Earth people can be delightfully responsive and receptive to the ideas and impulses of others. They are tirelessly supportive and would move heaven itself if that would get those they care about the things that they desire. They respond to the needs of others in practical ways, and you can be sure they will feed the hungry, clothe the naked, and shelter the homeless with joy and grace. These people endure. They have endless reservoirs of strength and, if they seem to move a little more slowly than other elemental personalities, they can be counted upon to be there for years—in season and out of season, helping others to deal with physical and emotional woes. Above all, the Earth personality's aid is sure to be useful and practical. Their solutions to any dilemma will be functional and they can be counted upon to discover practical shortcuts to anything from finding a job to getting a plumber. They do not like to waste their energy on theoretical speculation and prefer the tangible things in life. Not for them the vagaries of undue social intercourse to which the Water person is prone, or the Metal person's penchant for scaling the heights of theory and speculation. Earth people stand patiently by to tidy up the wreckage in the wake of a Fire person tracking his way like a comet across the night sky, and they make loyal administrators, working hand in hand with the corporate-minded Wood executive.

Like the Wood dominated, Earth people are excellent administrators. They are extraordinary in the sense that they not only organize a project, but work tirelessly to complete it. Steadfast and true, you can count on the Earth person to stay behind and finish something long after everyone else has gone home. Steady as they can be, however, Earth people are somewhat lacking in versatility—they are not jugglers of priorities or graceful acrobats in the realm of human endeavor. They like to undertake one project at a time. They get particular delight in accomplishing one task before proceeding on to another, particularly in the areas of tangible reality—money, real estate, or building. They are superb foundational people who function equally well in supportive or nonsupportive atmospheres.

Although they are sensitive, they are not particularily highly strung and can be depended upon to see things as objectively as any human being can. They are excellent at handling their own resources and those of others. Earth-dominated people often build hearty nest eggs with caution and reserve and invest them in ventures that pay off many times over. Hardly speculators or gamblers, they are nonetheless almost sure to make a profit and equally sure to spend their profits wisely. Moreover, they almost always give generously to those in need.

They methodically observe data, analyze information, and logically deduce conclusions uncolored by personal bias. The Earth mind approaches the world logically and methodically and will not embark upon any course of action without lengthy study and a host of good reasons. They never exaggerate and are honest and practical in their dealings with the more overt elemental signs. They do nevertheless expect the rest of the world to behave with the same clear-sighted conservatism, and therein lies the rub. Because the Earth-born are so cautious and careful by nature, they may have great difficulty in understanding why others insist on acting in such a variety of headstrong, willful, and generally foolhardy ways. If forced to exist in a circle of dramatic types, the Earth person will dig in his heels and become surprisingly stubborn and resistant to change. In his soul, the Earth personality distrusts change of any kind and will maintain to the last that he simply doesn't understand why all the upheaval is necessary. He does accept change, as long as it is of the slow, cyclic variety and proceeds according to those eternal and immutable laws of nature; but let's face it, havoc gives him hives. He can react physically to the disruption and unreasonable chaos caused by stupid things like people doing battle over pie-in-the-sky causes. No one hates injustice as much as he, but even more he hates poorly thought out, quickie solutions that create more problems than they solve.

He genuinely believes that it takes less time to sit down and ponder things for a while before acting on something. And even though he is sure to take the safest and best route for all, there are few who will not be driven to distraction by the fact that the Earth personality is, well, slow. And when some of the more adventurous types go charging off to their revolutions and battles and visions, he will bid them a worried goodbye, sigh heavily, and perhaps even feel a little sorry for himself, knowing that he is the one who will be left to clean up after their histrionics.

Still, he knows people must be allowed their idiosyncracies. He has immense compassion for others and a deep emotional identification with those in trouble or in need. He will not, however, dive in.

The Earth person can be as stubborn and immovable as a mountain when he has made up his mind, and no amount of pleading, cajoling, flattery, or threats is going to make any impression on him. Should he try to prevent you from embarking on a course of action he considers less than advisable, give up. Like the mountain, he will stand in the path of others on a more or less eternal basis—unless they take it into their heads to remove him stone by stone. Usually they won't. The prospect of changing an Earth person is just too daunting. It is much easier to tunnel through or altogether bypass mountainlike behavior. For this reason, in extreme instances, the Earth-born will find themselves abandoned by the very people they were trying to love and protect. But that doesn't mean that they are going to change their minds. Incredibly self-reliant, the Earth-born are quite able to keep themselves going with or without the help and support of others. In a peculiar way, they are extremely independent. It is much easier for them to help those around them than to allow others to help them even through the most perilous times. Besides, other people are rarely practical enough to actually be of much help to an embattled Earth personality. You want to help the Earth person, but just don't know how? Bring them a casserole or offer to do their laundry, but don't bustle over and offer to talk things out. These types loathe meaningful, touchy-feely emotional encounters.

This is not to say that the Earth-born don't feel. In fact, they are deeply emotional and usually very physical in their expression of affection. An

Earth-dominated partner may not necessarily show up with roses every Saturday night, but he or she can be counted upon to have your slippers at the door, a gourmet meal in the oven, and thick towels and bubble bath in the bathroom. They are marvelous lovers, perhaps not as passionately verbal as Fire types, or as electrically charged as Metal. They won't understand your psychic needs like Water creatures or regenerate you like the Wood-resonate, but they are thoughtful and considerate lovers and you can depend on them to be around the next day, the next year, and maybe even the next century.

If the Earth person can learn to loosen up a bit and stick more than his toes into the great ocean of things, he will probably do very well. Their greatest fault is their stubbornness and inability to change, and they must learn to accept that change is more or less inevitable. If they can manage to be just the teeniest bit flexible and not quite so constitutionally intolerant of more dramatic types, the rewards can be very great indeed.

Elemental Relationships

Before examining or attempting to interpret the different elements in a birth chart, it is important to understand the relationships between them and their creative and destructive effects on one another. In other words, it is not the elements themselves that are important, but their movement within the personality. The Scissors, Rock, Paper game is one good analogy for thinking about elemental relationships, but you might also try to think of the elemental cycle as a sort of spinning pinwheel, made up of five separate sections, constantly in motion. Each element of the pinwheel is a symbol for a transitional state or attitude that is eternally transforming itself into the next element. The principle of the pinwheel has been effectively used by human beings to construct windmills, waterwheels, and rotary saws, all of which use one or more of the five elements to transform the energy of another. It is the state of change itself that is important. The Five Elements represent certain forces in nature that describe (as we have previously stated) certain characteristics of the nature of energy as it makes itself evident in the world.

The first of the pinwheel's sections or areas is ruled by Metal, which contains and gives birth to Water. Water, the second section of the pinwheel, gives birth to Wood, which in turn fuels Fire, whose ashes make up the Earth, and Earth, in its time, gives birth to Metal again.

Yet just as pure energy can create and nurture, so it can destroy. Each element is seen by Chinese philosophy as having its destructive aspects as well, though destruction invariably gives rise to new forms of energy. Keep in mind that "destruction" in this sense does not have Western implications. Destruction is necessary to the creative cycle. In addition to being the instrument of change, the "destructive force" can also be seen as a mediating force, the means to channel rampant growth and focus energy into productive result. It's all a question of degree. Metal, for example, can be destroyed by Fire. Yet, at the same time, Fire can be used to melt and form Metal into useful things. It can burn off impurities and render Metal into a pure conductor. Fire can rage uncontrolled, but can also be extinguished or subdued by Water. Water is controlled by Earth, which can absorb it or hold it in reserve for times of drought when Earth is used to construct dams. Earth is depleted by Wood. The roots of the tree hold Earth close, and Wood draws Earth energy for nourishment. In the final component of the cycle, Wood is controlled by Metal—even the strongest Wood is felled or shaped by the Metal of saws or ax blades.

Under this system, we can see how all elements need to interact in order to present a clear picture of the movement of energy throughout the physical world. In a sense, each element requires interaction with other elements to reveal its energy in all of its forms. No one element by itself is better or more powerful than any other. In fact, the Chinese believe that the most fortunate people are those whose charts show an equal influence of each element. Although it is rare when such a configuration actually occurs, it shows the Chinese reverence for the qualities of each of the five elements and illustrates, too, that all the elements are irrevocably linked to each other, beginning and ending cycles of growth. Each has its place in the rhythm of the universe, each has its purpose and its function in human endeavor.

In interpreting the effects of various elements in one's chart, it is important to think about how the Five Elements work in the natural world. Then, once you have used the following methods to determine the elements in your own chart, think about ways to include elements that may be missing in your life. Augmenting your elements will be discussed in greater detail in Chapter 6, but it is often worthwhile for a person to surround him or herself with people whose charts include a predominance of elements the individual is lacking. Also, the characteristics of missing elements can be consciously developed and cultivated. A person with missing Wood, for example, might take it as a creative challenge to develop more organizational ability within himself.

Determining Your Dominant Element

There are a number of methods for determining the dominant element or elements of your Chinese astrological chart. Some Chinese experts assign a numerological value to each aspect, use date conversions, or assign varying values to each of the five determining aspects. For the purposes of this book, however, we have reduced a great deal of some complex methodology down to a simple formula, which results in an easy, accurate determination of your elemental status. What follows is a sample calculation of the Five Elements as present in one individual chart. The chart is then explored in a step-by-step procedure, followed by an interpretation of the elemental forces as they apply to the sample chart.

There are five factors to be considered in determining the dominant element or elements in the chart. They are:

The element of the year of birth
The element of the animal sign
The element of the hour of birth
The element of the month of birth
The element of the country of birth

At the end of this chapter, we have included five tables that provide ready access to the information necessary to determine the elements of your own or someone else's chart.

Our sample individual was born on June 12, 1953, at 9 P.M. in the United States.

The element for the year of birth, 1953, is negative Water. (TABLE 2-1)
The element for the animal sign, Snake, is negative Fire. (TABLE 2-2)
The element for the hour of birth, 9 P.M. is negative water. (TABLE 2-3)
The element for the month of birth, June, corresponds to the Western sign of Gemini and

the Eastern sign of the Horse. It's element is
positive Fire. (TABLE 2-4)
The element for the country of birth, the United
States, is positive Metal. (TABLE 5)

First, look up the element of the year of birth
on Table 1. Remember that the elements operate
in two-year cycles, first manifesting as Positive, or
Yang energy, then as Negative, or Yin energy. The
year of birth of our sample individual began on
February 14, 1953, and ended on February 2,
1954. It was the second year of the Water element
and therefore in a Negative or Yin manifestation.
It was preceded by a year of Positive (Yang) Water
(January 27, 1952 to February 13, 1953) and was
necessarily followed by a year of Positive (Yang)
Wood, (February 3, 1954 to January 23, 1955).

Next, look up the element of the Animal sign
in Table 2. In this case, the Animal sign is the
Snake. The elemental ruler for the sign of the
Snake is Negative Fire.

Third, find the element ruling the hour of birth
on Table 3. As in Western astrology, each Eastern
Animal sign rules certain hours of the day and
night, changing at two-hour intervals over a twenty-
four-hour period. The Chinese day actually begins at 11 P.M. Since our sample individual was
born at 9 o'clock in the evening, the ruling sign
for the hour of birth would be that of the Boar—
the last of the Animal signs, before the cycle begins again with the Rat at 11 P.M. In this case, the
elemental ruler for the Boar is Negative Water.

Next, locate the element for the month of birth on Table 4. In this case, the month of June corresponds to the Western sign of Gemini and the Eastern sign of the Horse. The Horse is ruled by Positive Fire.

Finally, locate the elemental ruler of the country of birth. In this case, the United States was "born" in 1776, the Year of the Monkey and the first year of a Metal manifestation. Therefore, the country of birth in this instance would contribute a Positive Metal element to the chart.

So, our sample birth information breaks down as follows:

1953 = Negative Water
Animal Sign (Snake) = Negative Fire
Hour of Birth (9 P.M. Boar) = Negative Water
Month of Birth (June, Horse) = Positive Fire
Country of Birth (U.S.A., Monkey) = Positive Metal

Take a pencil and paper and add up your elements, thus:

2 Water
2 Fire
1 Metal
0 Wood
0 Earth

The Chinese consider those born with some of each element to be the most fortunate, but in practice, this rarely occurs. Clearly, our sample case is lacking in Earth and Wood altogether, has but one Metal element, and is otherwise divided evenly between Fire and Water. The Chinese would attempt to balance this individual somewhat by adding to or even changing the name of this person with pictograms or characters to represent the missing elements, but since Western tradition doesn't allow for such liberties, we will first analyze the chart and then suggest ways in which this individual might compensate for the lack of certain elements in the birth chart.

Analysis and Interpretation

If you refer back to the personality profiles that precede this section, you will see that our sample individual is characterized by leadership, drama, and an outgoing nature, (Fire traits) coupled with intelligence, intuition, and fine communication skills (Water traits).

This person will doubtless experience an inner conflict between the impulse to charge fearlessly forward into those places where angels fear to tread and the desire to influence others in more indirect, subtle ways. There will doubtless be the strong desire to impose his or her will on others— much of the natural passivity of Water will be somewhat offset by the Fire's love of change for its own sake, a formidable ego, and an impatient, restless attitude toward slower personality types.

The presence of Metal in the personality makes this person his own best counselor. He bounces ideas off everyone in sight, (both Water and Fire are social elements), but ultimately he alone will be the one to decide on a course of action, though it will not be without some difficulty. This person is both reckless and impulsive on one side and highly intuitive on the other. When it comes to making up his mind, it is anybody's guess which side will win. Still, once a decision is made and a course of action charted, this individual will be surefooted and confident in the pursuit of his ambitions and goals.

Equally divided between Water and Fire, this is an individual who appears confident, cavalier, and even theatrical, but inwardly is sensitive and caring. Both Metal and Fire in the chart impart a degree of independence; this is not a person who is overly concerned about what others think of him. But he is nonetheless sensitive enough to respond to the needs of others in subtle ways. Always attuned to the inner content of any conversation, situation, or interaction, he soaks up impressions like a sponge, yet may never go so far as to mention them aloud. Rather, he allows his sixth and even seventh senses to inform his actions almost without realizing that he has done so.

This person is highly impulsive, and with the communicative skills of Water plus the oratorical passion of Fire, he is strongly verbal no matter what the circumstance. Should you get into an argument or debate with an individual of this type, be prepared to lose. Who is right may have little bearing on the outcome when you're up against a talker like this one. Yet for all of that, this person is not likely to be narrow-minded. Both Fire and Water appreciate new ideas and concepts and use those notions to inspire and influence others, if not to act, then at least to consider problems and situations in a completely new light. Also, whatever the issue, these are not people who express themselves and their arguments in strategic or objective ways. Everything is colored by a very personable quality here, though it would be unwise to mistake this personable quality as a true picture of real personality.

Our sample is highly skilled in social situations. Combined with the Animal sign of the wise and intelligent Snake, this person has no difficulty when others oppose his point of view. A master at overcoming resistance with charm and a magnetic appeal, he is unusually adept at bending people to his will. With the natural bravery of Fire and the natural diplomacy of Water, opposition means little to him.

Still, should our sample find himself in difficulty, he is far more likely to turn inward than to stand and fight to the last—the kind who is more likely to tear himself apart than to be torn apart by others. In fact, only the most perceptive among his closest friends and associates are likely to notice that something has gone awry with this individual. His anger is disguised under an aura of sociability, and his inner conflicts and problems are dressed up in theatrics and bravado. Don't be deceived by appearances here—what you see may not necessarily be what you get. However pleasant, social, and extroverted this person may seem to others, he is always dependent on a complexity of intuitive input. Underneath that cheerful, expressive exterior face may rage a whole, rolling river of emotion.

As we have seen, Earth and Wood are the administrative, organizing elements. Clearly, with a complete absence of those things, the danger for this individual is in spreading himself too thin. This personality has many friends and things to do, often too many to be really effective. He is easily bored and constantly reaching out in new directions, and there may be a strong tendency to dilettantism. Too, he may have trouble focusing his considerable energy, finishing projects, showing up on time, and may fritter away considerable intelligence, resources, and emotions by jumping from subject to subject or flower to flower. There is no Earth or Wood in the chart to channel the strong sensitivity and passion evident here, and this personality may get caught up in pure sensationalism. Metal will give some stability and endurance, however, provided that this person learns the value of his own counsel and company. If this individual allows himself the occasional retreat, and enough time alone, he can almost certainly learn discipline and perseverance, because Metal is the most focused of all elements. He may never, however, learn to like it.

In the natural destructive cycle, Water puts out Fire, so if this person allows his emotional, subjective side to dominate, he will almost surely be frustrated by his inability to impact on his surroundings. This is someone who needs to act as much as he needs to feel. As time goes on, however, the Water element can infiltrate, permeate, and eventually dominate the less desirable qualities of Fire. Remember, this is a Water Snake. Given time and the support of others, the reckless, destructive elements of Fire can give way to more nurturing impulses. The undiluted passion of Fire can be replaced by the more complex empathy of Water, and Fire's tendency toward oratory will be tempered by Water's ability to listen and evaluate. Ever a brilliant communicator, this person does best when he applies that talent to an appropriate field or profession. Above all, this personality must learn patience, receptivity, and discipline.

TABLE 2-1—THE ELEMENTS

This table shows the lunar years of each Animal sign from 1900 to the year 2000, followed by the element that rules those years. Note that each element rules for two years, manifesting first in Positive, or Yang energy, followed by a year manifested in Negative, or Yin energy. (A complete explanation of positive and negative energies with regard to the elemental cycle is given in Chapter Three.) Each complete elemental cycle takes ten years to complete (five elements at two years each) before the cycle begins again.

LUNAR YEAR

ELEMENT

January 31, 1900 to February 18, 1901.	Positive Metal
February 19, 1901 to February 7, 1902.	Negative Metal
February 8, 1902 to January 28, 1903.	Positive Water
January 29, 1903 to February 15, 1904.	Negative Water
February 16, 1904 to February 3, 1905.	Positive Wood
February 4, 1905 to January 24, 1906.	Negative Wood
January 25, 1906 to February 12, 1907.	Positive Fire
February 13, 1907 to February 1, 1908.	Negative Fire
February 2, 1908 to January 21, 1909.	Positive Earth
January 22, 1909 to February 9, 1910.	Negative Earth
February 10, 1910 to January 29, 1911.	Positive Metal
January 30, 1911 to February 17, 1912.	Negative Metal
February 18, 1912 to February 5, 1913.	Positive Water
February 6, 1913 to January 25, 1914.	Negative Water
January 26, 1914 to February 13, 1915.	Positive Wood
February 14, 1915 to February 2, 1916.	Negative Wood
February 3, 1916 to January 22, 1917.	Positive Fire
January 23, 1917 to February 10, 1918.	Negative Fire
February 11, 1918 to January 31, 1919.	Positive Earth
February 1, 1919 to February 19, 1920.	Negative Earth
February 20, 1920 to February 7, 1921.	Positive Metal
February 8, 1921 to January 27, 1922.	Negative Metal
January 28, 1922 to February 15, 1923.	Positive Water
February 16, 1923 to February 4, 1924.	Negative Water
February 5, 1924 to January 24, 1925.	Positive Wood
January 25, 1925 to February 12, 1926.	Negative Wood
February 13, 1926 to February 1, 1927.	Positive Fire
February 2, 1927 to January 22, 1928.	Negative Fire
January 23, 1928 to February 9, 1929.	Positive Earth
February 10, 1929 to January 29, 1930.	Negative Earth
January 30, 1930 to February 16, 1931.	Positive Metal

The Elements

LUNAR YEAR	ELEMENT
February 17, 1931 to February 5, 1932.	Negative Metal
February 6, 1932 to January 25, 1933.	Positive Water
January 26, 1933 to February 13, 1934.	Negative Water
February 14, 1934 to February 3, 1935.	Positive Wood
February 4, 1935 to January 23, 1936.	Negative Wood
January 24, 1936 to February 10, 1937.	Positive Fire
February 11, 1937 to January 30, 1938.	Negative Fire
January 31, 1938 to February 18, 1939.	Positive Earth
February 19, 1939 to February 7, 1940.	Negative Earth
February 8, 1940 to January 26, 1941.	Positive Metal
January 27, 1941 to February 14, 1942.	Negative Metal
February 15, 1942 to February 4, 1943.	Positive Water
February 5, 1943 to January 24, 1944.	Negative Water
January 25, 1944 to February 12, 1945.	Positive Wood
February 14, 1945 to February 1, 1946.	Negative Wood
February 2, 1946 to January 21, 1947.	Positive Fire
January 22, 1947 to February 9, 1948.	Negative Fire
February 10, 1948 to January 28, 1949.	Positive Earth
January 29, 1949 to February 16, 1950.	Negative Earth
February 17, 1950 to February 5, 1951.	Positive Metal
February 6, 1951 to January 26, 1952.	Negative Metal
January 27, 1952 to February 13, 1953.	Positive Water
February 14, 1953 to February 2, 1954.	Negative Water
February 3, 1954 to January 23, 1955.	Positive Wood
January 24, 1955 to February 11, 1956.	Negative Wood
February 12, 1956 to January 30, 1957.	Positive Fire
January 31, 1957 to February 17, 1958.	Negative Fire
February 18, 1958 to February 7, 1959.	Positive Earth
February 8, 1959 to January 27, 1960.	Negative Earth
January 28, 1960 to February 14, 1961.	Positive Metal
February 15, 1961 to February 4, 1962.	Negative Metal

LUNAR YEAR	ELEMENT
February 5, 1962 to January 24, 1963.	Positive Water
January 25, 1963 to February 12, 1964.	Negative Water
February 13, 1964 to February 1, 1965.	Positive Wood
February 2, 1965 to January 20, 1966.	Negative Wood
January 21, 1966 to February 8, 1967.	Positive Fire
February 9, 1967 to January 29, 1968.	Negative Fire
January 30, 1968 to February 16, 1969.	Positive Earth
February 17, 1969 to February 5, 1970.	Negative Earth
February 6, 1970 to January 26, 1971.	Positive Metal
January 27, 1971 to January 15, 1972.	Negative Metal
January 16, 1972 to February 2, 1973.	Positive Water
February 3, 1973 to January 22, 1974.	Negative Water
January 23, 1974 to February 10, 1975.	Positive Wood
February 11, 1975 to January 30, 1976.	Negative Wood
January 31, 1976 to February 17, 1977.	Positive Fire
February 18, 1977 to February 6, 1978.	Negative Fire
February 7, 1978 to January 27, 1979.	Positive Earth
January 28, 1979 to February 15, 1980.	Negative Earth
February 16, 1980 to February 4, 1981.	Positive Metal
February 5, 1981 to January 24, 1982.	Negative Metal
January 25, 1982 to February 12, 1983.	Positive Water
February 13, 1983 to February 1, 1984.	Negative Water
February 2, 1984 to February 19, 1985.	Positive Wood.
February 20, 1985 to February 8, 1986.	Negative Wood
February 9, 1986 to January 28, 1987.	Positive Fire
January 29, 1987 to February 16, 1988.	Negative Fire
February 17, 1988 to February 5, 1989.	Positive Earth
February 6, 1989 to January 26, 1990.	Negative Earth
January 27, 1990 to February 14, 1991.	Positive Metal
February 15, 1991 to February 3, 1992.	Negative Metal
February 4, 1992 to January 22, 1993.	Positive Water

LUNAR YEAR	ELEMENT
January 23, 1993 to February 9, 1994.	Negative Water
February 10, 1994 to January 30, 1995.	Positive Wood
January 31, 1995 to February 18, 1996.	Negative Wood
February 19, 1996 to February 7, 1997.	Positive Fire
February 8, 1997 to January 27, 1998.	Negative Fire
January 28, 1998 to February 5, 1999.	Positive Earth
February 6, 1999 to January 27, 2000.	Negative Earth

TABLE 2-2—ANIMAL SIGNS AND FIXED ELEMENT

Each Animal sign has a fixed element and a positive or negative stem. You will notice that no Earth elements are represented in this table or in those for months and hours of birth. Each of these aspects is governed by the elemental ruler of its corresponding Animal sign. According to the Chinese system, this is because the elements of the Animal signs, of necessity, relate to Earth. Any Earth elements in the chart will be derived principally from the year of birth. If, however, you were born in the year of the Ox, the Dragon, the Sheep, or the Dog, you should take into account that many sages considered these signs to have Earth as a secondary element, and should study the section on Earth for relevant clues to your personality.

SIGN/ELEMENT

Rat, Positive Water
Ox, Negative Water
Tiger, Positive Wood

SIGN/ELEMENT

Rabbit, Negative Wood
Dragon, Positive Wood
Snake, Negative Fire
Horse, Positive Fire
Sheep, Negative Fire
Monkey, Positive Metal
Rooster, Negative Metal
Dog, Positive Metal
Boar, Negative Water

TABLE 2-3—ELEMENTS OF THE HOUR OF BIRTH

The elements of the hour of birth are determined by the governing Animal sign of the time of day.

SIGN HOURS	ELEMENT
Rat—11 P.M. to 1 A.M.	Positive Water
Ox—1 A.M. to 3 A.M.	Negative Water
Tiger—3 A.M. to 5 A.M.	Positive Wood
Rabbit—5 A.M. to 7 A.M.	Negative Wood
Dragon—7 A.M. to 9 A.M.	Positive Wood
Snake—9 A.M. to 11 A.M.	Negative Fire
Horse—11 A.M. to 1 P.M.	Positive Fire
Sheep—1 P.M. to 3 P.M.	Negative Fire
Monkey—3 P.M. to 5 P.M.	Positive Metal
Rooster—5 P.M. to 7 P.M.	Negative Metal
Dog—7 P.M. to 9 P.M.	Positive Metal
Boar—9 P.M. to 11 P.M.	Negative Water

TABLE 2-4—ELEMENTS OF THE MONTH OF BIRTH

The elements of the month of birth are determined by the governing Animal signs. The Chinese calendar, because it is based on the movement of the moon rather than the sun, is somewhat different than the Western calendar. If the element assigned to the month you were born does not seem appropriate in the resulting natal chart, and you were born after the twentieth day of any given month, read the element assigned to for the following month. Included are the weather and environmental conditions ruled by the months and elements, because the individual will respond to those conditions in any given season.

MONTH	SIGN	WEATHER TYPE	ELEMENT
January	Ox	Winter/Cold, Wet Weather	Negative Water
February	Tiger	Early Spring/ Cold, Moist	Positive Water
March	Rabbit	New Growth/ Warm, Moist	Negative Wood
April	Dragon	Vernal Equinox/ Clear, Warm	Positive Wood
May	Snake	Early Summer/ Hot, Moist	Negative Fire
June	Horse	Summer Growth/ Hot, Dry	Positive Fire
July	Sheep	Summer Solstice/Hot, Moist	Negative Fire
August	Monkey	End of Summer/ Hot, Dry	Positive Metal

MONTH	SIGN	WEATHER TYPE	ELEMENT
September	Rooster	Early Fall/ Dry Cool	Negative Metal
October	Dog	Autumn Equinox/Dry, Cool	Positive Metal
November	Boar	Winter Begins/ Cold, Wet	Negative Water
December	Rat	The Snows/ Cold, Wet	Positive Water

TABLE 2-5

COUNTRY OF BIRTH	ANIMAL SIGN	ELEMENT
United States	Monkey	Positive Metal
England	Sheep	Negative Earth
France	Dog	Positive Earth
Canada	Rabbit	Negatie Fire
USSR	Snake	Negative Fire
China	Ox	Negative Fire
Israel	Rat	Positive Earth
Hong Kong	Tiger	Negative Metal

Chapter Three

INTERPRETING YOUR ELEMENTS IN RELATION TO THE ANIMAL SIGNS

Most modern books and manuals on Chinese astrology determine the dominant element of the horoscope by using only the year of birth. For example, on our sample chart, anyone born June 12, 1953, would be considered by most modern practioners to be a Water Snake, because he or she was born in the year of the Snake during a negative Water manifestation. But, as we have already discovered, to interpret this person solely as a Water Snake gives a less than accurate picture of the personality, since it is evident from the chart that there is a strong element of Fire as well as some Metal to round out the picture of our sample's personality.

Our sample was admittedly a complicated one

from the interpretive point of view, but it is in just such cases that the interpersonal skills and intuition of the astrologer come into play. Yet, many will find that a majority of birth charts often point to a clearly dominant element and the task of interpretation will be rendered that much easier.

But whatever the elemental picture a birth chart presents, it must always be interpreted in relation to the individual Animal sign. Both elements and Animal signs are intimately related to one another and to concentrate on one without the other is likely to give a lopsided picture. In a sense, the elements are the qualifiers of the Chinese chart. The dominant element or elements in a chart can be seen to color, add dimension, and in effect, personalize a chart, much in the same way that a Western astrologer uses the ascendant, time zones, and moon signs. And it is just these factors that spell the difference between an individual profile and reading one's horoscope in the newspaper.

The personality signs that follow give an indication of the effects of the various elements on the Animal sign. If, like our sample, you are more or less evenly divided between two elements, read the description of each of the Animal sign personalities relating to your own element configuration. You may find one or the other predominates in your personality. For more information on dominate and conducive elements to help you in interpret- ing your personal chart, refer to Chapter Four.

THE FIVE TYPES OF RAT

The Metal Rat

The combination of Metal with the sign of the Rat is bound to be successful. The normally emotionally contained Rat personality finds it easier to express his emotions as he gets older, because the elemental movement here is from Metal to Water, the Rat's natural element. While young, however, this type of Rat appears very self-contained. Metal makes the Rat physically strong, and can channel his nervous energy into athletics. Also Metal strengthens the Rat's naturally caring nature, imparting high moral standards and expanding him ideologically. This is a naturally accumulative type, capable of earning, saving, and investing money in very imaginative ways. This is someone who is both intellectually and emotionally nurturing to those around him, but the loner aspects of Metal always seem to be in some conflict with the Rat's gregarious, social nature.

The Water Rat

There is no conflict here between the natural element of the sign and the dominant element. This type is highly emotional and communicative, but the natural practicality of the Rat prevents him from ever being a purely emotional type. More likely, he will seek to structure his wealth of emotions and interests through scholarship, study, and intellectual pursuits. This is someone who gets along with everyone, and is capable of understanding and communicating with a variety of people. Undoubtedly many great teachers are of this type. The Animal sign of the Rat is always practical; his instincts keep his emotionalism in check and prevent the double Water configuration from spreading out in too many directions or succumbing to the empathetic passivity that sometimes can define the Water dominated. They must, however, be careful to keep their intense inner emotions in check and be conscientious about finding constructive outlets for their nervous energy. Nonetheless, this type makes it his business to know all the details of everybody's personal life, and makes a best friend and confidante.

The Wood Rat

In the natural cycle, this is a conducive combination—Water gives rise to Wood. The Rat combines well with Wood; both are highly industrious and energetic. This type likes organization and administration and is able to get the best out of others in practical ways. This is not a theorist; his goals are workable and detail-oriented, and his approach to those goals is be flawlessly thought out. The Wood Rat is more emotionally expressive than his Rat fellows. But there is a tendency toward anger and frustration when things don't move according to plan. This is someone who can profit by learning to lose some of his cool, detached exterior and yell and scream on occasion.

There is an inner conflict between Wood's natural confidence and expansiveness and the Rat's commonsense approach to the world. The Rat is a worrier and with this configuration will almost certainly suffer some sleepless nights on the subject of whether or not events are spinning out of his control. He is less conventional than his counterparts.

The Fire Rat

Fire makes the Rat less cautious than his brothers and uses the Rats nervous energy to generate activity. These Rats are enthusiastic but are quarrelsome and unpredictable. Their problem is actually within themselves; Fire and Water are in conflict internally but the gregarious Rat expresses his unease externally with all the passion and fireworks of the combustible element that rules his chart. They may also be demanding, and in more undeveloped types there is less here than meets the eye. Although they have dramatic exteriors and no end of oratorical ability, in everyday life they are thrifty, methodical, and systematic. This Rat is independent and may very well change his life and circumstances overnight in temperamental Fire fashion. But rest assured the pragmatic Rat has weighed the pros and cons of any sweeping change before applying it to real life.

The Earth Rat

Water and Earth make this Rat implacable and imperturbable on the surface, but passionate and sensitive underneath. He values stability, security, and home life above all else. He is motivated by awards and recognition, but his methodical pursuit of success and stability may make him secretly terrified of change. It is this Rat who will have to be pried out of his rut. The practicality of Earth and the industriousness of the Rat native can be combined into an effective thrifty manager. They are equally liable to be stodgy sticks in the mud. The nature of this Rat more than any other depends a great deal on the quality of the personalities with which he or she surrounds themselves. These are the great homebodies of the Rat family, people who have a place and use for everything and for whom everything must be in its place. Earth can serve to suppress Water sensitivity here. This Rat is not one to spread himself out in all directions. He is single-minded, reliable, and nurturing. He forms long-term alliances with others. Earth administrates Water's emotional sensitivity.

The Five Types of Oxen

The Metal Ox

The element of Metal shortens the patience of the Ox while paradoxically increasing his stubbornness. The creative aspects of Metal combined with the Ox's inborn element of Water make him artistic, eloquent, and perhaps more intelligent than other members of the Ox family. This Ox relies to a great extent upon his intuition and is less objective than some others of his clan. Metal gives the Ox boundless ambition, particularly where career matters are concerned. The Metal Ox can be argumentative; Metal augments the natural communicative powers of Water and, when combined with the Ox's obstinancy, may make him unwilling to accept other viewpoints. Nevertheless, this is a highly reliable Ox, self-sufficient and resourceful. He takes himself and his world seriously and may have melancholy moods. In the Metal Ox, logic is combined with vision. Their industriousness is contagious—the Metal Ox is nothing if not charismatic. Although this person does a fair amount of service in the interest of others, he is always personally ambitious. He is loyal to a fault, however, and remains steadfastly helping those whom he has chosen to love until death do them part. Although not always demonstrative, the Ox is warmer than other Metal-dominated Animal signs.

The Water Ox

The Ox is in his natural element here. He is more sensitive to the emotions, thinking, and opinions of others and takes the viewpoints of others into consideration. He is more sensitive than other elemental Oxen and, although not innovative, he is more flexible, diplomatic, and subtle. He demands the most of himself and expects others to do the same. However, Water's empathy should not be interpreted in this native as tolerating weakness or self-indulgence in others. Tolerant they are not. Water is more focused in this Animal sign and its energies are channeled through hard work, commitment, and a certain reverence for tradition. Although this type of Ox is as slow to accept the new as any other Ox, there is more likelihood of gradual change taking effect over time, in a kind of "as water weareth away the stone" dynamic. Water Oxen are less prone to nervous disorders and breakdowns than other Animal signs dominated by Water, and they can also nurture others while they themselves are undergoing hardship. They can communicate well emotionally but never let the emotions of others sway them. Slowly and persistently, they sway others to their way of thinking and doing things.

The Wood Ox

The most innovative and likely to achieve prominence in life, this Ox uses the natural ability of Water to bring into flower the administrative and artistic abilities of Wood. He has a genius for managing others simply because he does so without pretension or demand. More sociable than other Oxen, this native has a wider range of personal and business contacts and his energy is all but inexhaustible, both in endurance and intensity. This Ox looks up from the yoke long enough to appreciate the future and plans to use it to his advantage. But this combination will bring the fabled Ox temper to the fore. Combined with easily angered Wood, the Ox temper can turn downright frightening. And in the throes of a tantrum, this Ox wreaks long-lasting havoc and destruction. Conscious of other people's feelings but oddly unable to express his own, the Wood Ox would do well to release his more volatile emotions in physical exertion. The natural physical strength of the Ox combined with indefatigable Wood energy produces a daunting combination. He is not self-effacing as other Oxen, either. He is confident of his ability and place in the world, but he may not be as expansive as members of the other Wood elementals. He does his best when overwhelmed and has the stamina and good humor to shoulder the burdens of others with joy and grace.

The Fire Ox

By far the most combative of all Oxen, the Fire Ox is at war with his own sensitive element, Water, as well as the world at large. He can be more forceful and proud than other Oxen and may even fall victim to a superiority complex, which is rare for an Ox member. Particularly in early life, when the qualities of Fire are most prominent, this Ox seems harsh in his dealings with others. There may be a sarcastic or sardonic quality in the way he expresses himself. He is the least patient of all Oxen and may also be the least considerate. Nonetheless, he is honest to a fault, if not exactly diplomatic, and will never be caught taking advantage of others. Highly protective of his family and loved ones, who benefit most from this Ox's labors, he is at his best with a cause to fight for. He helps those around him more than he manages to help himself. He is a superb military person, lawyer, or union leader. The Fire Ox does not mind the fact that he can't always labor for himself, he would rather right the world's wrongs than worry about his personal problems. As he ages, he mellows. The Fire traits give way to a greater understanding of why people behave in certain ways, and if he is not exactly tolerant, he is fearless and sure to rise to any challenge presented.

The Earth Ox

Although Water and Earth provide a nurturing basis, this is the least creative type of Ox. These natives are loyal, steadfast, and sincere. He is almost sure to do well in any career he undertakes because he patiently does whatever needs to be done to assure his advancement and security. He is practical and industrious, a methodical planner who is determined to a fault. You will never find an Earth Ox retreating, wandering aimlessly, or surrendering any ground he has gained. This Ox is receptive to the needs of others and gives support and understanding. He is also a materialist of the highest order and expects to enjoy his comfort once he has earned it. What he lacks in versatility he makes up for in single-mindedness of purpose. He works slowly but tirelessly, and his patience is inexhaustible. He can be appealed to in his rare Ox rages through logic, as long as it is an honest attempt to contribute to a solution and not a game. He has a superb sense of justice and is generous to those in need. Intensely compassionate and devoted, this Ox expresses his love in physical ways. He is self-controlled and dedicated, if somewhat lacking in humor; reliable and comforting, if a little dull.

The Five Types of Tiger

The Metal Tiger

Wood and Metal combine in this Tiger to form an extremely aggressive, passionate personality who will stop at nothing to get to the top. His attitude is cheerful and optimistic, and he is untroubled by some of the more melancholy emotions of Metal. Others respond to his glamor and even allow this Tiger to exploit them on occasion. He is a risk-taker and he derives endless delight from doing those things that would horrify a fainter heart. Wood and Metal make him constantly expanding, devoted to his own interests, and hooked on instant gratification. To this Tiger, an imperfect world is simply not an acceptable option. Never try to impose well-meaning advice on him. Not only will he refuse to listen, he will trample you in his rush to get away. Whatever this Tiger's flaws, you can depend on him to be successful and active. Even when he has achieved his goals, he is not the kind to sit and bask in the glorious glow; he is sure to be off to the next task—even if it promises to throw all his accomplishments in jeopardy. This is not a Tiger who is overly concerned with relationships, and not the kind to sit down and iron out any problems, either. If things aren't right, he is more than willing to go his way alone. He can, however, be depended upon to find an unorthodox solution to each and every problem, and will see it through, for better or worse, in an untiring and enthusiastic way. Headstrong doesn't even come close to describing this personality. As a Tiger, he may fall victim to niggling self-doubt upon occasion, but with Water and Wood, such doubts will not last long. This Tiger needs channeling of his energies, but it is not a task for weaker types.

The Water Tiger

Water and Wood combine in this personality to form an open-minded person, constantly on the lookout for new ideas and experiences. In fact, the Tiger in him will perish if there is not enough new input to keep him stimulated. The Water element heightens his subjective, personal intuition, but Wood here serves to objectify that information as he applies it to the world. This is a calmer type of Tiger, able to perceive the inherent truths in people and situations around him. The sensitivity and organizational ability of Wood keeps this Tiger from taking risks for the thrill alone. He has great intellectual ability and can wait and plan to get what he wants. Although the Tiger in him is still freedom-loving and dramatic, Water and Wood help him to temper the drama in practical ways. He is good at promoting other people and their ideas and at public relations. He is also good at motivating freedom-loving types because he understands them. Like all Tigers, he has a tendency to put things off because he doesn't feel like attending to them and enthusiastically explores all kinds of tangential rabbit trails if he senses a new idea or experience. Still, he is less temperamental than other Tigers, more reasonable, intuitive, and a difficult person to fool. When unjustly angered, however, be forewarned that this is the most wrathful and vengeful of all Tigers. Water dilutes the Tiger's natural cheerfulness and optimism somewhat, and when angered this Tiger is sure to hold a grudge until he feels the score is settled.

The Wood Tiger

Here the Tiger assumes the personality of the house cat. He is affable, tolerant, charming, and affectionate. He has many friends and associates, some of them from unlikely walks of life. Remember, All Tigers like variety, but the Wood Tiger loves innovation. He is democratic and fond of bringing together different types of people, personalities, and ideas. He can be superficial; his considerable intellectual abilities allow him to correctly assess people and situations at a glance, and he rarely wants to delve much further. Like the house cat, he remains aloof when he chooses. He doesn't concern himself with the grand passions of life or have much in the way of fierce emotional dedication. The expansiveness of Wood, together with its managerial skills, make this a Tiger a bit too adept at delegating responsibility. He may be so good at getting others to perform for him, that he fails to pull his share of the load. This Tiger thrives on attention and admiration and requires a certain amount of petting and pampering—he usually gets it. The Wood Tiger does not excel at self-discipline or self-denial. This Tiger has a sizable ego; he does best when surrounded by those who know how to flatter and cajole him toward achieving a particular end. Equally, he is likely to revolt against outright criticism or the pointing out of his limitations. If push should come to shove with this Tiger, he'd rather leave and find someone who will appreciate him than take advice or admit his faults.

The Fire Tiger

This type of Tiger is dramatic, theatrical, and imposing. The Tiger's natural element of Wood gives way before Fire, and so this type is less given to administrative abilities and being a team player. He has many excellent leadership qualities, provided he can settle down long enough to speak out for a group or cause. His is a restless, transitory nature, however, and it may be that he only hangs around long enough to incite and inspire less theatrical types before moving on to the next idea. Nonetheless this Tiger is generous and giving. He has boundless energy and enthusiasm and is never duplicitous or two-faced. He is socially and professionally popular and will always be surrounded by a group of admirers. This is not an objective Tiger. All of his associations are highly personalized and he proves himself to be genuinely caring about those with whom he associates. Fire combines here with the farsighted qualities of Wood, and this Tiger can be counted on to be unconventional and innovative, whatever his course of action. Rest assured, this Tiger will act—he values action above all things and is often not choosy where his actions take him. This is the sexiest of Tigers—they seem to exude a magnetism and sensuality that is hard to ignore. Not for them, however, anything resembling the tortured romance. They completely avoid pessimistic emotion or Water-influenced introspection and empathy. Fire, Wood, and the Tiger all point to extraordinary resourcefulness. Whatever the circumstance, they move others to action, and others love them for it.

The Earth Tiger

Earth makes this Tiger more steadfast and resolute than his Tiger brothers, and less prone to undue risk taking. Earth and Wood make him more analytical, clear-headed, and objective. Both Earth and Wood impart the ability to work and plan, and this Tiger is likely to be corporate- or organization-minded. But the Tiger's natural charisma will guarantee him a place at the top of the corporate ladder. This is a Tiger who likes the tried and true. In fact, he may even be a little afraid of that Tiger hiding in his heart. He may even be the kind "who protests too much," insisting on the most circumspect and conservative conduct from himself and others. Whatever his impulses, this is one Tiger you won't find on the cutting edge of the avant-garde, but despite himself, his natural uncoventionality ends up shining through. Once this Tiger has gone through his paces and made it to the top, he may surprise everyone by fueling a scandal or two. This person takes himself very seriously until he has gotten where he wants to go, and then cuts loose in some downright shocking ways. It is true he is conservative, but only to a point. In positions of power, this Tiger can seem very hard on others—he is a difficult taskmaster, and will make absolutely sure that everyone does their part. The Earth Tiger is a truth seeker; he uses logic and an objective viewpoint to arrive at his unique and sometimes eccentric views of the world.

The Five Types of Rabbit

The Metal Rabbit

The Rabbit's natural element is Wood and in combination with Metal, this Rabbit is more of a loner than his fellows. He has enormous faith in himself and little tolerance for those who do not share that faith. His exterior always remains unfalteringly polite, if a bit on the chilly side. He is passionate when emotionally moved, and is most likely to be moved by beauty, works of art, and the more refined side of things. This Rabbit is difficult to understand; the expansiveness of Wood is in conflict with Metal's solitary nature. Nonetheless, he is sensitive and highly intelligent. He makes an excellent critic or connoisseur. He has inborn taste and an unerring eye for quality. Wood makes this Rabbit farsighted and Metal makes him visionary. He knows, without hesitation, which artists and their works make the best investments, and which will rise to prominence in the future. This Rabbit is a hard worker and immensely talented. He may reveal his gifts early in life and can have the potential to be a child prodigy. He is able to read people with the same unerring vision with which he reads works of art. But he is not the kind to express his judgments readily. The Rabbit is a tolerant type, and sincerely believes that others should be allowed to follow their own paths. In relationships, the Rabbit is a bit aloof. He does not bond easily with others, but when he does form a close association, he proves himself incredibly loyal and true.

The Water Rabbit

Both Water and the Rabbit make this individual very sensitive. He is highly attuned to the vibrations around him, and although not personally passionate he can find himself overwhelmed by the emotions of those around him. He requires a peaceful, harmonious environment, surrounded by the beautiful things that Rabbits hold dear. Others are often drawn to this Rabbit; he wakes up their altruistic tendencies and their desire to help. But, chances are, this Rabbit will always remain somewhat emotionally conflicted, no matter who his champions or how great his security. This Rabbit is prone to all sorts of emotional episodes and even breakdowns. They are simply too sensitive for their own good. They can be psychically gifted, even though they may sometimes be unwilling to express their feelings about things, perhaps because they are afraid of the repercussions. The Water Rabbit can nurse an injury for a long, long time. When wronged, this Rabbit can become positively obsessed with hindsight. They are very much aware of their natural passivity when conflict is at hand and afterward can quite easily succumb to the treacheries of "what might have been" and, "if only I had . . ."

The Wood Rabbit

Wood plus Wood makes this Rabbit so sympathetic to the needs of others that he is likely to deny himself. He is concerned with the virtues of the status quo and may be too lenient and tolerant in dealing with the mistakes and transgressions of the more dramatic Animal signs. He is not decisive and he can see all sides of any issue so clearly that it may be almost impossible for him to make up his mind. The Wood Rabbit needs to be part of a structured group and can contribute to a corporation or institution in subtle, graceful ways. He is, like all Rabbits, a gifted diplomat. Wood plus Wood makes him extraordinarily conscious of the needs and perspectives of others. This native is flexible, accommodating, energetic, and able to fit in with any group or circumstance. He is adaptable, although double Wood as well as his Rabbit sign makes him seem a little impersonal, even in emotional relationships. Yet, in reality, he is more emotionally secure than other Rabbits. Wood plus Wood gives him a strong ego and can make him vain. The artistic inclinations of the Rabbit combined with double Wood draws him most certainly to the visual arts. This Rabbit has one of the most discerning eyes, and his natural taste and discrimination can give rise to some very refined and creative work. This is practical art at its best—not for the Wood Rabbit is the dramatic work of the Tiger, Dragon, or even the Snake. Pleasant, popular, and wise, this Rabbit has only to take care that he doesn't become a pushover. He is likely to do well in almost anything he undertakes.

The Fire Rabbit

Fire and Wood in the Rabbit native make him extremely emotional and, unlike the other Rabbits, completely unafraid of expressing his emotions at every opportunity. He is more demonstrative and affectionate, and has a singular fondness for the occasional, rip-roaring good time. Fire here may make him seem more temperamental, but the natural Rabbit charm imparts an ability to get his way without Fire's general messiness. The Fire Rabbit is a little less formal and aloof than any of the other Rabbits. He is also more easy-going and looks elegant in his shirtsleeves. He is a natural leader, outgoing and progressive in thought and action. Given the outward strength of this character, any enemies will be more prone to use subterfuge than to provoke him to direct confrontation. Like all Fire types, this Rabbit requires the complete support and backing of his friends and partners in order to do his best. He is prone to flattery, although the Rabbit in him accepts it for what it is. The influences of Wood make the inspiration of Fire in this sign more practical. The Fire Rabbit can plan and stick to his plans in ways other Fire signs are unable to do. He is detail-oriented and even more intuitive (because of the Rabbit's characteristics) than other members of the Wood element.

The Earth Rabbit

Earth in this Animal sign makes the Rabbit more deliberate and less likely to give in to his natural inclinations. He is realistic and pragmatic in his approach to life and does not spend as much time in the world of abstracts as either the Metal or Water Rabbit. He is not as highly strung, either. An Earth Rabbit is extraordinarily self-reliant, able to keep himself going for long periods of time without the help of others. Independent and nurturing, this Rabbit cares for others in practical ways. He is, however, an introvert and, when under siege, will go within himself in order to deliberate before choosing a course of action. The materialism of Earth combined with the Rabbit's love of beauty are sure to make his warren a beautiful and sensual place. He will not, like other members of the Rabbit clan, disappear at the first sign of conflict. He was made for the long haul. Earth and Wood combined with the Rabbit sign make this person extremely detail-oriented. Sometimes he is not able to see the forest for the trees. His steady charm makes him appealing to those he meets, and the Rabbit's natural elegance makes him more stylish and adept at social relations than the other members of the Earth element.

The Five Types of Dragon

The Metal Dragon

Metal combines with Wood here to form a tough, hearty Dragon with a stronger will than any of his fellows—which, in the Dragon clan, is saying a great deal. Every bone in this dramatic Dragon's body is an honest one, and these natives are exceptionally straightforward. Their love of action may make them aggressive, and they are not adverse to confrontation or even outright attack. Metal and Wood give the Dragon logic, efficiency, and an enormous capacity for work. This is a Dragon with little patience for fripperies, foolishness, or dishonesty. His is a warrior's nature. He will take up the banner for any reason at all, even a bad one, as long as he is convinced that the cause is right. Metal and Wood combine here to make for a formidable adversary. He can, and will, crush the opposition with little regard for the sensitivities and sensibilities involved. The Metal Dragon is visionary and theatrical. He can inspire others with his flair and insight, and his natural expressiveness draws people to him like a magnet. This is an intense combination with an enormous ego. When opposed, he can be the absolute epitome of righteous indignation. He will advance his cause or die in the attempt; retreat, in this individual, is tantamount to dishonor. His sense of good and evil is highly developed and though he will undoubtedly be blind to the necessary shades of gray in the world, he is a champion of truly heroic potential.

The Water Dragon

Wood plus Water makes this Dragon an excellent negotiator. He can calm the waters, smooth ruffled feathers, and iron out the wrinkles in any situation while at the same time providing for the good of everyone. The intuitive powers of Water make him wiser than the other Dragons, whereas Wood makes him progressive, logical, and able to build for the future, as long as he takes care to build on solid ground. This is an extremely creative Dragon, and this quality will reveal itself in all that he undertakes. The hardest thing for this

Dragon is to learn to let go, when it has become obvious that he's made a mistake. This native, unlike his fellows, will not be offended nor bear a grudge if others do not follow his leadership. He has a highly developed sense of self and rarely depends on others to validate it. He loves admiration, but does not require it. The Water Dragon is just as opinionated as any other Dragon but, unlike his brothers, will not feel quite so compelled to impose those opinions on others. Water here is diplomatic and accommodating, but not necessarily passive. Cool and collected, this is a Dragon who is quite capable of taking his own path until others realize just how right he has been all along.

The Wood Dragon

Wood plus Wood makes this Dragon the most successful at working with others. Both the Dragon and Wood are innovative and respond well to new ideas. If no new concepts are to be found, be assured that he will come up with a few ideas of his own. This Dragon is curious about everything; he can form lofty theories and airtight theses from the flimsiest evidence. He loves logic and the workings of the mind, yet is invariably intensely dramatic. The danger here is to become lost in the machinations and details of things. Never get into an argument with this Dragon; if he can't bowl you over with theatrics, he will wear you out with nitpicking. This Dragon has a massive ego. No matter what his capacity for logic, he will almost surely find a way to relate anything back to himself. He is, however, generous and anxious not to offend anyone. He does try to hide the fact that he's basically domineering by convincing others that to agree with him is ultimately in their best interests, and he will compromise on occasion, when duly convinced that it is for the good of all. Wood and the Dragon prove doubly lucky in making and attracting money. People invest in his ideas because he is so honest, but also because his ideas are usually characterized by their ultimate workability.

The Fire Dragon

If you can manage to walk through the flames, you will find this person to be warmhearted, honest, and inspirational. But Wood plus Fire plus the Dragon makes this one prone to spontaneous combustions of all kinds. He has absolutely no patience, is critical, and borders on the despotic. Temperamental and proud, this Dragon is demanding and authoritarian in all his dealings. Yet, underneath his fiery exterior, this Dragon is curiously humane. His demands do not seem at all unreasonable to him, and are simply his way of getting others to toe the line. He is very ambitious and a total perfectionist. This Dragon, unlike the others who tend to form lifelong attachments at relatively young ages, fall in and out of love easily and intensely. But, given the fact that a relationship with a Dragon of this type is likely to be difficult (to put it mildly), his torrid alliances may not be very long-lived. Sooner or later, this is a Dragon who will be in the public eye. He would do well to learn a little humility, or at least to express his views in less threatening ways. If he can manage this, the Fire Dragon will be the most magical of all Dragons, none of whom are short of sorcery.

The Earth Dragon

Other Dragons may strive to be warriors or kings, but Earth in combination with this personality's natural element, Wood, makes him an executive par excellence. Earth makes him more inclined to team effort than to solitary quest. He is fair-minded and methodical, willing to listen to the ideas and opinions of others. He is not in a hurry to get where he is going. He knows his is the right path, and he takes time to smell the flowers along the way. He still needs to administrate and control, but Earth gives him more stability and Wood and Earth give him an eye for the tried and true and the future good of all. He is self-reliant and resourceful, and Earth and Wood combined with the Dragon's natural energy enable him to work long, intense hours for the good of whatever group he has decided to head. The Earth element gives him the appearance of being less rushed and frenetic than other Dragons. But this hardly means he is lacking vision or dedication. He approaches things simply and does not complicate his life with the usual Dragon theatrics. Like all Earth types, he is self-controlled and reasonable. Earth lends the Dragon stability but, just because he is steady as a rock, don't expect him to lack vision or imagination. All Dragons are imaginative on a grand scale. This native believes dignity is all. If his dignity is offended, he is quite capable of letting loose a volley of fire that will decimate his opponent. He tolerates weakness in others, but when the time comes, he will cut off without a backward glance. Earth in this Dragon nurtures, but only when his wishes are carried out. He is extremely pragmatic and that attitude extends to any and all of his relationships with others.

The Five Types of Snake

The Metal Snake

Metal combined here with Fire, the Snake's natural element, makes this Snake the most self-sufficient of all. This Snake, like all Snakes, is attracted to the realms of power and influence, but Metal's vision can take him to the inner circle long before anyone else is even aware that he's around. This Snake can be a schemer, but the need for power is pervasive and all-consuming. Second only to power is his love of money and accumulation, which is equally important to the wise and wily Snake. This person is incredibly enthralling and mysterious, but strangely unable to communicate. Metal always marches to a somewhat different drummer, and the Snake is forever inscrutable. If you're expecting this individual to sit down one of these days and really open up a garrulous, heart-to-heart conversation, you could find yourself waiting a very long time. The Snake always retains its enigmatic character, and coupled with Metal, these natives doubtless communicate most effectively through a kind of subliminal message. Others resonate and respond to this Snake, but without quite knowing why. Metal Snakes make artistic business executives and businesslike artists. They bring an ineffable style to all their pursuits. Whatever they do, however, they are sure to make a lot of money and get to the top in a very short time. This Snake is suspicious; they are so complicated themselves that they tend to expect others to be equally so. The Metal Snake can be generous and cooperative, but he is so self-protected and guarded that others rarely see his offerings as not having strings attached.

The Water Snake

Water makes this Snake one who will communicate more easily than some of his brothers. He is intensely psychic, because both Water and the Snake are highly intuitive. The Snake's natural element, Fire, makes him more dramatic and less passive than other Water types. Yet Water makes the Snake even more insidious and able to penetrate obstacles or opposition. Others find the Snake mysterious and alluring, the Water Snake knows how to turn those qualities to his advantage. He can make others want what he wants, with little or no overt effort. Despite his sensitivity and psychic abilities, though, this is one Snake who never loses sight of the practical side of things. He is a good manager of people, resources, and money. This Snake's instinct for power sources draws him to managerial positions of all kinds and enables him to infiltrate almost any power structure. Fire draws him to grand schemes and designs, and Water gives him the power to see them through. Despite his flair for the practical, the Water Snake is likely to find himself drawn to the arts, where he will find a natural outlet for his wisdom and ability in music or literature. Any art this Snake creates will be highly complex, emotionally evocative, and tightly structured. This Snake is superintelligent and he will doubtless apply that intelligence in practical ways. Here, however, the languid mystery of the Snake masks a brain that is always working, calculating, and putting ideas together with the speed and precision of a computer. He misses very little and stores his data for ages. Be warned: this is a deadly Snake when roused and has a long, long, memory for injuries. But no matter how angry, the Snake always chooses his moments. If you have crossed him, you can bet he will strike back. You just won't know when.

The Wood Snake

Wood in this sign makes this Snake able to shed his skin easily. He uses the intuition of the Snake for growth that benefits not only himself but those around him. He is farsighted and more objective than other Snakes. The Snake makes the Wood element here more inclined to form close personal relationships, as long as he is allowed complete intellectual freedom. Wood and Fire make this Snake's intelligence sympathetic and resonant to broad sweeps of history. The movement of people and events can be viewed by this individual in patterns that affect the past and future of world events. For this reason, the Wood Snake is a strangely accurate prophet, although he will not necessarily suggest emotional solutions, or make wild predictions regarding the future of the planet. The Wood Snake, although he may still find personal expression difficult, excels at public speaking and logical thought. Like the Water Snake, he attracts people to him easily and many of them will be fascinated by his Snakelike mystery and charisma. When people have been around him long enough, they discover a kind and wise person, but this takes time. His is not an easy personality to get to know. Wood and the Snake combine to make an enlarged sense of self-importance in this individual, and he can be quite vain.

The Wood Snake has a genuine need to be surrounded by the best of what life has to offer and is a devoted promoter of all the arts. He can apply the knowledge gleaned from his tireless information gathering in practical terms and, unlike many other signs of the Wood element, is less prone to overexpansion. Whatever the Wood Snake decides to build will last. Wood gives him more endurance as well. Whereas most Snakes (with the exception of the Earth Snake) tend to work in energetic bursts followed by rest (during which, however, they never stop thinking, planning, or creating), the Wood Snake is more consistent in his work patterns and his approach to his goals.

The Fire Snake

Fire is at home in this sign, because the Snake's ruling element is Fire. This makes for a great natural leader and, like all fiery personalities, he is dramatic and appealing. The Snake makes him form intense personal attachments, but this Snake can become closed off within a small circle of close associates, because he tends to be rather suspicious by nature. This Snake can be exceedingly self-involved; his emotions run to excess, but he may never betray a troubled heart to the world. This Snake is even more attracted to power than other Snakes, which is saying a lot. Accumulation also figures strongly here, and whatever his path in life, this is one Snake who is unlikely to fall. He can capture the imagination of large groups of people—his is a personality that can be invested with the ambitions and dreams of many. Everyone has a tendency to see exactly what they want to see in this individual. In reality though, he is less of a deep thinker than other Snakes. He is more of a symbolic sort of leader than a hands-on administrator. Because of this unique ability to capture the public imagination, this Snake may make a lot of enemies. There are always those who will be critical of popular icons—but this is unlikely to bother the Fire Snake. His supporters will always poutnumber his critics. Double Fire will not show itself to be as destructive, theatrical, or strenuous as in some other Animal signs. The Snake is by nature subtle and refined, and his wisdom will keep Fire under control.

The Earth Snake

The Earth Snake is graceful and controlled. He is more immediately appealing than others of his clan, because he is more personable and perhaps not as mysterious. Sensual and calm, he is the most approachable of the Snakes and perhaps the most friendly, at least on the surface. The charisma of the Snake is rendered more personal here, and sometimes more effective as well. This individual would make an excellent teacher or counselor, because he functions brilliantly in small groups or in one-on-one situations. The natural ambition of the Snake is translated in this type into a remarkable ability to take charge in any crisis or difficult situation. People trust the Earth Snake's calm and cool efficiency and react to his inner wisdom and steadfast qualities. Where other Snakes invariably inspire admiration, the Earth Snake inspires loyalty. Conservative with money, like all the Earth dominated, he is equally hardworking. Not as fitful in their approach to what they want, Earth Snakes have an intuitive ability to assess situations and people. This Snake keeps his own counsel; he is never influenced by public opinion. Earth imparts to the Snake's natural Fire common sense and a powerful self-knowledge. He knows who he is and where he's going, and although his ambitions may not take him to the upper echelons of power like his fellows, he is sure to succeed.

The Five Types of Horse

The Metal Horse

Metal combined with the freedom-loving Horse make this the most headstrong and irrepressible of the lot. The finely honed intuition of both Metal and the Horse, together with the energy of Fire, give this native insight, intellectual ability, and a fascination with new concepts and ideas. Both intuitive and logical, this Horse requires constant intellectual stimulation and bores easily around slow thinkers. This person loves the challenges inherent in life. Once he has achieved his goals or overcome a specific set of obstacles, he is off and running to the next set. This is one Horse that will lie down and die if he is restricted in his freedom. He thrives on danger and often seeks it out, undertaking some foolhardy risks purely for the thrill of doing so. Sexy and physically strong, the Horse radiates an exuberance that proves irresistible to others. But he may be easily spooked by the threat of real involvement, fearing that his freedom will be curtailed. Almost nothing fazes the Metal Horse—he is protected by a tough ego and a sense of adventure. By definition a ground-breaker, he may fail to see things through, simply because he lacks the patience for detail work and steady application of his talents. He is instead a pioneer par excellence. His own dislike of rules and regulations give him a certain outlaw quality, and his own love of liberty makes him hesitant to restrict others. The Horse makes him less melancholy than other Metal types, probably because he expends so much physical energy in the course of his day that he has little left for undue introspection.

The Water Horse

Communicative Water merged with the optimism of the Horse and the natural verbosity of Fire combine to give this Horse a brilliant sense of humor. The sensitivities of Water and the Horse give this native a sixth sense for danger and when he scents it in his path, he will switch courses without breaking stride. This type is so adaptable that others may find it difficult to keep up with him. Like all Horses, he has great reserves of physical energy and needs to keep active if he is to remain healthy. Above all, this Horse must act. He is a little lacking in analytical ability and believes that circumstances can be changed sometimes just by changing the scenery. He makes an excellent businessperson, but his deals are always be made with an eye to his own best interests. This Horse could learn much from Wood-dominated people about long-range planning and sticking to goals. He is sometimes too skittish about commitment to be effective at anything. Emotionally, this Horse lives on his nerves. He is not nurturing, though he is generous with his time, money, and resources. But if a problem cannot be solved with what this Horse has to offer in terms of tangible help, that problem is likely to go unresolved. He does not have the patience for long discussions, introspection, and analysis.

The Wood Horse

Wood makes this Horse more logical and cooperative with others than the rest of his clan. He has a naturally optimistic attitude, and a wide and influential circle of friends and associates. All Horses are marked by a sense of humor, and this trait combined with Wood makes him an entertaining and thoroughly witty conversationalist on almost any subject. He is not competitive, and will gladly assist others in their rise up the ladder, providing their ideas are innovative enough to have captured his imagination. He adores change and, although he'll branch out in Wood fashion, he will shoulder an extraordinary amount of responsibility—for a Horse. This Horse is a fine networker and has little trouble gaining the support and interest of others because of his unusual charm and enthusiasm. He is intensely energetic and is willing to work hard for his beliefs and causes, but he can be easily seduced by mere novelty and could learn to be somewhat more discerning. This is the original work Horse—he is realistic and quite responsible, but not as intuitive as some of his brothers. Emotionally, this Horse is rarely depressed and, aside from the inherent Horse tendency to be restless and generally high-strung, he is happy and even-tempered.

The Fire Horse

Double Fire makes this Horse a thoroughbred, in the best and worst senses of that word. Just as a thoroughbred can be beautiful, a delight to the eye and mind, he may also be temperamental, fragile, and good for one thing—running. This Horse captures the imagination of all who behold him, but prolonged exposure to this firebrand can be very difficult indeed. In Chinese tradition, the Fire Horse is considered singularly unfortunate, especially for women born under this configuration. Women so born were thought to make unruly wives, in whom the traits of domesticity and service were nonexistent. It was further believed they would compound the error of their ways by outliving their husbands and bringing shame to his family through their terrible tempers and willful attitudes. Although the situation is not that serious in contemporary societies, this Horse can nonetheless be an unmanageable character. He won't take direction from anyone, much less a superior, and is likely to rear up and trample anyone who gets in his way. This Horse is physically powerful and all but immune to danger, but his high-strung nature makes him susceptible to the least distraction. He does, fortunately, have a singular gift for getting himself out of trouble, but it is matched by an equal talent for creating it. If this Horse can learn to go the distance and keep his mouth shut, he can effect constructive change.

The Earth Horse

Earth in this sign tempers the extravagance of Fire and serves to stabilize the Horse's high-strung temperament. Although not as imaginative as other Horses, this Horse will use any available resource to construct a solid foundation for his dreams and plans. This type uses his Horse-sense to discern good investments and solid financial deals and is likely to provide for his own security. Unlike other Earth types, he breathes fresh air and new life into stodgy traditional systems. He won't go charging off into the unexplored like other Horses; he has to weigh the pros and cons of every decision first. This Horse exhibits his skittishness and sensitivity in a compulsion for detail. The kind to conceal nervousness under seeming calm, he'll drive those around him wild as he insists on counting his penny collection during an argument. Unlike other Horses, the Earth Horse does not mind having other people tell him what to do. He can function very well within an established system or structure, but always does so with a number of little signature quirks or eccentricities—keeping his own hours, painting his office a particular garish shade, or insisting on engraved business cards, when the rest of the company carries embossed. Once this Horse has his mind set, however, he may take on more of a resemblance to the mule in his stubbornness and endurance in an argument. Persuade this one with carrots and sugar rather than the crop and all is likely to go smoothly.

The Five Types of Sheep

The Metal Sheep

Metal combines with the Sheep's natural element of Fire to make a Sheep with great self-confidence and aplomb. Blessed with a somewhat more secure sense of self than others of his clan, he still has the Sheep's sensitivity and vulnerability, but is able to disguise his feelings behind a courageous attitude toward the world. The Metal Sheep has a finely honed sense of beauty, and Metal adds to his already highly developed sense of the artistic. Above all, it is important for this Sheep to be surrounded by beautiful things, for it is from such things that he derives a sense of security. Once gained, however, he may toss security aside. This is a Sheep who feels compelled to challenge himself. It is as if he is aware of his own tendencies to passivity and timidity, and is constantly trying to prove to the world at large that he was overcome these things. And it is this quality that can make the Metal Sheep, (like all Metal-dominated types) his own worst enemy. This native may even be a little too successful at disguising his sensitive nature under a rough-and-ready veneer. There are those who are put off by his seeming careless independence and fail to discern this

Sheep's emotional side. Metal and Fire combine to make this a highly emotional sheep—he is susceptible to mood swings, possessiveness, and periods of melancholy. And yet he is equally likely to have a perverse sort of attitude toward his emotional attachments. This Sheep is difficult to get close to. Some fail to see that his insistence on total independence in relationships is a plea for deeper loyalty or that his casual attitude toward attachment may mask the need for genuine affection.

The Water Sheep

Water in this sign makes the Sheep even more sensitive than he would be normally. All the intuitive powers of Water are brought to bear, making this Sheep even more aware of the motivations and problems of others. Unfortunately, he may also have a tendency to become absorbed in his own emotions, and may very well end up internalizing the emotional ups and downs of those around him. Although Fire gives him an appreciation of new ideas, Water and the Sheep sign leave him fearful of change. But the Water Sheep is tremendously appealing and others will be unable to resist his pleas for help, knowing that he is kind and gentle. When the Water Sheep is in trouble, he is never alone for long. He attracts rescuers and guiding lights and is loyal and true to those who help him out—as long as they don't tell him how to behave. No matter how much trouble the Water Sheep is in, he does not take kindly to strong-arm techniques. He is far too sensitive for this type of treatment. He does his best when his champions encourage him and bring out his talents. The Water Sheep worries even more than the rest of the Sheep clan except, perhaps, the Earth Sheep, and can make life quite miserable for others with his pathetic bleating if he is not constantly shown the sunnier side of life. He can be counted upon to complain, even if he is happy. The Water Sheep may be the proverbial wet blanket; he can physically influence others like all Water-dominated types. Water makes him less likely to buck the status quo, even though the Fire element here encourages him to get his own way in oblique and circuitous ways. He has a positive terror of the unknown and may suffer and whine miserably rather than take a risk. Still, he is able to make friends with almost anyone and tends to forget his own trials and tribulations when other people are in trouble. As long as there is a stronger personality present to beat away the undeserving from his door, he can be among the most empathetic, helpful, and kind counselors around.

The Wood Sheep

The resourcefulness of Wood combined with the Fire element in the sign of the Sheep makes this individual less helpless than his Water-dominated brother. He has a tendency to see the brighter side of things as well; both Wood and Fire are optimistic elements. Wood gives him a strong ethical backbone that helps to channel the empathetic Sheep nature into positive action. He will help those in need in practical as well as emotional ways. But he still has a tendency to give in to stronger elemental and Animal-sign types in order to create a peaceful existence for himself. Close friends are amazed to discover that he trusts them implicitly. He extends himself to taking in all kinds of animals and humans who are down on their luck. Those chosen by him for special attention may, however, feel smothered by his ministrations. But they can be relatively certain he will never want anything in return. Wood and Fire make him extremely compassionate, and he manages to find the money and resources he needs to support his strays. No matter how big his heart, however, this is not necessarily a person who will do missionary work in the Third World; the Sheep in him still resists new situations. He is much more likely to be found quietly, tirelessly working in his neighborhood. Wood gives him stamina and a concern for the concrete injustices of the world. He wants to help people in specific ways. Although the Fire has him agonizing over wider ecological concerns, he rarely becomes an activist in theoretical causes.

The Fire Sheep

Fire is at home here in the sign of the Sheep, and this Sheep is more stalwart and courageous than other members of the flock. He acts on his intuition without first weighing the pros and cons, and can start and finish projects by himself if no one shows up to help him. The natural creative abilities of the Sheep manifest themselves here in an ability to expand and develop ideas once someone else has come up with them. He can make the wildest ideas appear feasible and oddly logical. Even at his most dramatic, the Sheep in him tends to make his ideas and concepts peaceful and comforting. Double Fire, however, exacerbates the natural Sheep tendency to overspend and overextend himself. This Sheep likes to be surrounded by elegant trappings, along with people affiliated with collection agencies. He dislikes reality and may in his more negative states be unable to handle practical life problems. He is also prone to bouts of emotional histrionics. He would do well to have his affairs managed by a more money-oriented sign, or by someone who is Earth dominated. He is not above fighting for what he believes in, and is much more energetic than other Sheep. People are attracted to his gentle, graceful oratory and the emotional understanding he offers, but he utterly refuses to suffer fools, and he has less patience for the unfortunate than the Wood- or Water-dominated Sheep. He can be a bit of a dreamer, particularly when deprived of his creature comforts, which he regards as necessities of life, and he strenuously resists those who try to force him into considering harder realities. He does not respond well to charity, either. Fire makes him independent and sure of his own path in life. He would do well to develop logical approaches to problems and curb his tendency to emotionalism when things don't go his way.

The Earth Sheep

Earth makes this Sheep more optimistic and less prone to bouts of self-flagellation and worry. Perhaps this is because this Sheep is an emotionally steadier type and one less likely to get himself into precarious financial binds through chronic over-spending and excessiveness. Nonetheless this Sheep never denies himself the finer things—Earth loves his comforts as well as the Sheep. Rather, he plans for the purchase of his luxuries and, once acquired, delights in them for years to come. The Earth/Fire combination here makes this a physically strong Sheep, with lots of endurance. This type can work all day and play all night with no ill effects. Caring and sociable, this Sheep takes the world seriously, without undue personal suffering. He is always there for those in need and can be quite a soft touch. The acquisitive qualities of Earth are somewhat modified here. This type genuinely likes to make money and can be quite gifted at doing so, but he is not a penny-pincher. He is more generous than other Earth types and, curiously, less concerned with issues of security than either his fellow Sheep or other Earth-dominated personalities. This is the original "easy come, easy go" personality. The downside to this personality is that he is more sensitive to personal criticism than any other Earth type. Too much well-intentioned advice can turn this individual neurotically defensive—someone who more resembles a porcupine with his quills up than the normally calm and placid sheep.

The Five Types of Monkey

The Metal Monkey

The power of Metal is doubled here, making for a Monkey that is superintelligent and one of the quickest studies of the Chinese calendar. Endowed with the ardent zeal of the Metal-dominated, this Monkey is more likely to stand and fight than to talk or otherwise wriggle his way out of difficulty. He can turn argumentative when the strength of his convictions comes into question. Perhaps because of this quality, this Monkey does best when self-employed. He does not take direction from others kindly and has little patience for those with slower minds, whether or not he happens to be working under them. In this Monkey, independence can be taken to an extreme. His formidable analytical qualities can lead him to the frequent conclusion that he is simply smarter and better equipped to deal with situations than anyone else, and although that can certainly be true, it is not an attitude that makes for great team players. This Monkey makes an excellent and wily entrepreneur with a knack for making and investing money. He would make a great salesman—especially if his product is innovative or ingenious—or an equally successful speculator. It is the Monkey's nature to gamble and this configuration gives him the proverbial "nerves of steel." The Metal Monkey is more demonstrative than his fellows. Emotional associations with this character doubtless have a whirlwind quality, both because of his ardor and the speed with which this type can approach any objective.

The Water Monkey

This is a harmonious configuration, making for a cooperative person who will nevertheless keep an eye out for his own interests. The naturally gregarious Monkey is made more so by the element of Water, but he has a secretive side and is hesitant to reveal his inner feelings. In a way, he is more comfortable when observing the dynamics of human interaction than he is when forced to participate. This is a sensitive and caring Monkey endowed with a great degree of understanding and patience for the follies and foibles of others. Water makes the Monkey less superficial and may give him a greater sense of purpose, as this configuration will slow him down enough to be better able to grasp the inner workings and potentials of his personality. Like all Water-dominated signs, this Monkey has a knack for motivating others. He is marked by the ability to venture original and ingenious opinions and gain support for them with little personal effort. The Water Monkey has a great deal of style. Just as he strives to present his views in the best and most appealing light, so he will be similarly blessed as he presents himself to the world. At its most negative, Water makes the Monkey hypersensitive; he takes offense easily and may get even with his offenders in cruel and clever ways. He knows how to wring the most out of situations and can be notoriously fickle. Yet, it is this same instinct that can make him a great negotiator or go-between.

The Wood Monkey

Wood coupled with Metal makes this Monkey a brilliantly gifted communicator. In fact, it may be impossible to shut him up and let the rest of us squeeze in the occasional word edgewise. There is a strong ethical sense here, which works well for the Monkey and prevents him from turning overly meddlesome and prying into the secrets and affairs of others simply for the thrill of discovery. Wood does much to focus the Monkey's unstable qualities, and gives him the ability to plan in practical ways. Conversely, the Monkey gives Wood a clever aspect that it may lack ordinarily, and imparts to Wood a lighter heart and greater sense of play in its approach to the world. Unlike many Wood types, the Wood Monkey is friendly and approachable. This Monkey has more natural endurance than his fellows and is less susceptible to burnout and boredom. Both Wood and the Monkey like to problem-solve, and this character is extremely resourceful. With Metal as the Monkey's ruler, chances are the problem will be identified, analyzed, and resolved before anyone else even knew it had arisen. His finely honed instincts make him a wonderful troubleshooter, whereas his verbal abilities and Wood's sensitivity to the larger good make him equally successful at avoiding compromising situations. Although he may appear friendly, however, this Monkey is not of the more personable variety. Like all Wood types, he may be difficult to get to know, perhaps because his mind and mouth are moving so fast. But more frustrating still is the sense that he has not taken time to get to know those he loves, either.

The Fire Monkey

Fire combined with the Monkey's natural element, Metal, make this a person torn between leading the world on to discovery and making his own way. Fire forces the Monkey to be taken seriously; he is the most competitive and driven of his clan. This character's combination of Metal strength and Fire passion creates a powerful person with a dominant, aggressive personality. He knows what he wants and he's determined to get it, although the Monkey will see to it that he may be somewhat inconsistent in his procedure. Fire makes this Monkey visionary; he is likely to be more original than other types, but his passion may run away with him if it is not kept in check by more dependable friends. Fun-loving and dynamic, this Monkey's ego is nonetheless huge. He can be a formidable adversary if he feels he has been passed over. He can also be surprisingly petty and vindictive. Like all Fire types, he has an inborn need to beat everyone else at the game, and gaming is the Monkey's motivating drive in life. He has to be Number One. In this instance, the grand designs of Fire have all the willpower of Metal behind them. In his rise to the top, this person can be powerful and imposing, but he wants to have a good time along the way. He is extremely controlling and expects others to follow. This is perhaps due to his complexity and a certain paranoia. He thinks that others are as devious as he is and he is certain that life is not what it seems to be on the surface. Fire gives this native even more luck than the considerable store Monkeys generally possess. He can be a fearless speculator as well as a charming gambler, but this is one Monkey who will make a fool of himself if his speculations are not well-founded. He loves invention and uses new things to tantalize the interest of others: He expects everyone to be as curious as he is. He is also quite capable of dazzling others with his fancy footwork.

The Earth Monkey

The Earth element in the Monkey's sign is sympathetic to the natural Metal element. All Monkeys are clever, but the steadiness of Earth can make him an intellectual. He is studious and serious with a singularly un-Monkey-like predisposition for thoroughness and a highly developed sense of duty. He is less flighty than other Monkey types and bears a natural sense of integrity, which is not as moralistic as that of the Wood Monkey. Monkey gives the Earth element a mental rather than physical dimension, as well as an objectivity in dealing with others. He makes his demands for appreciation more quietly than other Monkeys, but if he is not admired, he is inclined to massive bouts of sulking. This is not a Monkey who expresses himself in shrieking tantrums like some other members of his clan. He has a scientific bent, rare in Monkey natives, who are generally more interested in social interaction. He has the ability to persevere through years of tedious experiment in order to prove his ideas valid, and Monkey problem solving here translates into patient and methodical and scientific method. Curiously, this Monkey is less social and not as fond of hectic schedules, chaos, parties, and disorganization. He is not easily diverted from his concerns and prefers a quiet life surrounded by creature comforts. Earth Monkeys will almost certainly acquire a great deal of material goods and are true philanthropists, but they prefer to write checks rather than become personally involved and definitely strive to keep the rabble out of their own backyards.

The Five Types of Rooster

The Metal Rooster

Double Metal makes this Rooster a real stickler for detail. Exacting of himself and others, this is one of the most willful and headstrong types. He has truly brilliant powers of deduction and an undeniable personal flair that is sure to captivate those around him, providing they are not put off by his somewhat eccentric exterior. Metal is a loner, and since the Rooster finds it difficult to compromise, there is a danger here of being rigid and unbending. Emotional and passionate as he is bound to be, this individual will nevertheless find it difficult to express his more intimate feelings. He is very vulnerable and somewhat insecure beneath the brave and persnickety face he shows the world. Like many Metal types, he may show himself to be fiercely independent just when he is neediest. This Rooster could have an almost clinical streak and subject even his nearest and dearest to overanalysis and his all too critical scrutiny. He is not impossible to get along with, but remember that the surest way to this Rooster's heart is through his ego. This type must be mollified and his ruffled feathers smoothed before he can ever be reasoned with. Confrontation with this character should be avoided whenever possible. If you've ever witnessed a cockfight, the reasons are obvious. Roosters are always combative and, dominated by Metal, they can turn positively ferocious when their views or beliefs are challenged. This Rooster is passionate about his work, and does well in those professions that best utilize his investigative talents and penchant for detail. Orderly and precise to a fault, Metal also attracts him to notions of social reforms. This type is not without sympathy for the suffering and downtrodden, and he could also do well in hospital work, or administrative medicine.

The Water Rooster

The Water Rooster is clear thinking and less excitable than his Metal-dominated brother. The most intellectually inclined of the Roosters, he is fond of the arts and culture, and somewhat better equipped to join in cooperative efforts of all kinds. This Rooster doubtless has a considerable talent for writing—Rooster gives him the necessary patience for detail and Water imparts to his character a genuine desire for communication. Water dominated, this Rooster is likely to be more sympathetic to the needs and emotions of others, but his Rooster-like preoccupation with detail and his systematic approach to problems may very well defeat his purpose. He has a highly developed sense of what others "should" do with their lives, and, if not kept in check, the Rooster's superior attitude could be very obnoxious indeed. The Water Rooster is not as passive as other Water types, however, and there is less of Water's tendency to be all things to all people. Water does well by the Rooster—it does much to soften his somewhat didactic approach to things and also serves to make him less demanding and more social. There is still a danger of obsessing over the details of life and using his love of systems in less than constructive ways—Chinese water torture was undoubtedly the brainchild of a Water Rooster. But this is, ultimately, a more reasonable Rooster than most, and surrounded by the right influences and people, one who can be highly effective and successful.

The Wood Rooster

The natural kindliness of Wood can give way before the Rooster's natural element of Metal and the results will not always be positive. This is a highly controlling character—he is doubtless a lean, mean administrator, but hardly a joy to work for. He is likely to obsess over those lunch hours that run two minutes long, send detailed memos on the subject of paper waste, and spend his off-work hours dreaming up ways to reorganize the employee parking lot. Needless to say, this Rooster is enthusiastic and progressive, as long as he is careful to use those energies wisely and channel them in constructive ways. Wood integrity is unpolluted when paired with Rooster honesty. This individual is completely trustworthy and, remarkable in a Rooster, will not be tempted to tell all he knows as soon as he knows it. He tempers his critical faculties with understanding in this configuration and Wood sociability offsets the Rooster's eccentricity and standoffishness. He has a fine social conscience as well, and is happiest using his talents and resources to improve world conditions in practical rather than theoretical ways. He is more humanitarian than other Roosters and less inclined to defeat his own purposes through erratic action, overcriticism, and sheer bossiness.

The Fire Rooster

Fire plus Metal combined with the crowing eccentricity of the Rooster make this a visible native in any crowd. He may appear odd in thought and mannerisms, but there is an electric quality about this character that makes him attractive and convincing despite first impressions. Fire makes him less detail-oriented than other Roosters, and even more concerned with capturing the limelight. This is not difficult, because he is an exciting and stimulating person to be around. He bubbles with new ideas and is adept at furthering the interests and talents of others upon whom he relies for creativity. This is a person who gets things done as quickly as possible. He can land himself in devastating predicaments, but he does not care how others perceive him and he has enormous powers of resilience. He can attract loyal followers because he has a professional way of dealing with dramatic situations, despite the fact that a great deal of the drama may be self-inflicted. He must be on the cutting edge of his art or business and will only diminish his energy if he feels he is not consistently breaking new ground. His boundless enthusiasm inspires others to produce for him, and he is good at managing people because he has the ability to encourage them and keep them focused when their interest begins to lag. He must have his own way, however. Should things not go according to his plan, he becomes extremely picky. The Rooster is a natural nag and Fire in this sign tends to escalate this particular trait. He has a tendency to relegate any problem to microscopic investigation and once he has decided on a course of action, he becomes remarkably rigid. If he can learn even a little diplomacy and develop flexibility, there is no end to what this Rooster can accomplish. Oddly enough, he is a loner and resents having to justify or explain himself to others: He has thought out his actions in his orderly Rooster fashion and he believes that should be enough. He can be a loyal friend who will wear away the opposition, Rooster-fashion, bit by bit. The Rooster here gives Fire some stability, but both signs are inveterate talkers, and even quiet Roosters born in a Fire year have quite a lot to say. He is relentless in his criticism of those whom he considers enemies; not only does he hold a grudge, but he voices it loudly from whatever rooftop he happens to be sitting on at the moment.

The Earth Rooster

At first glance, this person may not seem to be a Rooster at all, until you realize that his penetrating glance hasn't left your face for forty-five minutes or longer. On closer inspection, you realize there is something a little odd about his haircut or that his jewelry, although small and tasteful, is actually quite bizarre. Earth gives this Rooster more steadiness and the insightful quality of Metal is translated into an obsession with practical detail. Practical with him means alerting you first and foremost to the bottom line and drawing it to your attention at every opportunity. Rooster outspokenness is softer here—this person will be of few words but you can be sure that every one of them will be blunt. He is determined to change the world but avoids the histrionics of other Roosters. However, he likes to keep extensive notes on his life—for his autobiography, of course. He knows that he will make a difference in the world and that others will want to be inspired after his death by his stellar example. Earth and Metal give him an endless well of energy and the Rooster applies this energy methodically. His files and record-keeping systems are perfect and his mind retains detail upon detail. He can get the most out of others, but he is not as sympathetic as other Earth elements. He is an inspired critic, but one who probably overlooks the positive qualities of the person, idea, or work that he is critiquing. He believes the purpose of criticism is to point out areas that need improvement and not to advance an incorrect view. He is better than most Roosters at taking on enormous responsibilities, and he doesn't necessarily need recognition for his contribution. At least not right away. Earth gives this Rooster more grace in his movement and physical presence, and his voice is not so strident. This person can cut to the heart of a problem, but once he has, he expects others to sit up, take notice, and act on his advice and observations.

The Five Types of Dog

The Metal Dog

Metal, at home in the Metal-ruled sign of the Dog, makes this person even more loyal and determined than other Dogs. But double Metal in this sign produces a Dog of extremes. Like the little girl in the nursery rhyme, the Metal Dog is very, very good, but when he's bad he's horrid. He is, however, noble and idealistic to a fault, willing to undergo great trial and tribulation on the side of what he feels is right. He can be selflessly dedicated to worthy causes or wholeheartedly obsessed with tracking down and destroying his enemies. Double Metal gives the Dog an extra dose of wide-ranging vision, which he expresses in strong social and political ideals. Whatever the issue, he is never indecisive. Fence-sitting is anathema to the Dog, and more so in this expression of his sign. This Dog imposes stern personal discipline and an exacting mental regimen on himself, and he expects others to do the same. The natural sexiness of the Dog becomes breathtaking in this Metal combination, but others will never be able to seduce him, unless he is so inclined himself. He doesn't play around and is devoted to his loved ones. He may think less of others who try to get him to indulge in sensuality for its own sake, because he regards this as a character weakness in a personality who has not managed to control his or her emotions. He puts the needs of social groups before his own and yours. Should you find your-self in an argument or conflict with this character, give up. The righteousness of his point of view, combined with his convincing Metal verbal skills, will win every time. His noble character and hu-manitarian instincts probably make him right, and prolonged disagreements with this native will be a lot harder on you than on him. He won't give up until he has won, even if he's the only one left alive to enjoy the victory. Rose-colored glasses are not for the Metal Dog. He has an unem-broidered view of people and a suspicious nature, but his so-called realism never extends to his lofty ideals.

The Water Dog

First and foremost, tradition holds that natives of this configuration are among the most beauti-ful and sensual of the Chinese calendar. Dogs are naturally sexy creatures and perhaps the legend-ary empathy and psychic appeal of Water gives that extra added something necessary to turn heads and break hearts in all quarters. Whereas the Metal Dog is characterized by his rigidity, the Water Dog can be characterized by his liberality. Perhaps in keeping with their sexy appeal, these Dogs have gained an equal reputation for promiscuity. At the very least, however, they tend not to form intense personal bonds, sometimes sacrificing the fabled Dog loyalty for the sake of self-gratification and adventure. They are more easygoing than other Dogs, and less likely to turn their talents to social reforms and championing just causes. Water also makes this native less suspicious than some other types. His Watery intuition enables him to better understand and appreciate the motives of those around him, and although he may bark and snap at an adversary, he is less likely to draw blood. Water-dominated Dogs are not as prone to self-absorption and extreme emotionalism. The Dog is always a little cynical and this gives Water a little healthy distance on itself and its problems. Water and the Dog make him superintelligent and highly perceptive. He is likely to be more contemplative than other Dogs and will be able to come up with an insight or two on the meaning of life. The Dog in him sees things fairly, whereas Water enables him to see all sides. He can weigh the pros and cons of an issue with sensitivity, and still remain objective.

The Wood Dog

This is the truly self-made Dog. Wood and Metal combine here to render this individual popular and charismatic, highly devoted without the obsessional qualities of Metal. He does, however, like to run with the pack and, hard as he may work to develop himself in life, he could do well to learn a touch more independence and not be so concerned with the opinions of others. This Dog responds to nature and the outdoors and needs a beautiful environment in order to be able to do his best. Although Wood encourages expansion and progress in material realms, the idealism of the Dog protects him from becoming too acquisitive or greedy. This Dog naturally attracts all different kinds of people, and is equally willing to listen to all points of view. He is assertive, but always in a socially graceful fashion. Both Wood and the Dog are intensely energetic, but this character is most likely to channel his energy into partnerships or groups, rather than solitary pursuits. He requires social contact and is likely to be quite unhappy if left on his own for long. Wood and the Dog are both honest and ethical in the extreme. When others show themselves to be lacking in those areas, this Dog turns his disappointment into aggression and, although he may not cut all ties, his relations will never be the same. This Dog can be a legend in his own time, providing that his nature is not purely conciliatory, and that he can invest his natural honesty and idealism with the strength of true conviction.

The Fire Dog

Fire in this Animal sign assures this Dog his position as the Leader of the Pack. Fire lends the Dog a friendly sort of drama, and Metal gives Fire the strength of application and conviction. Like the Water Dog, this individual is likely to be popular with the opposite sex, but in a less mysterious and alluring sort of way. Fire makes him utterly unafraid of involvement with others, but he most definitely wants to be the dominant party in any relationship. Here the Dog's egalitarian streak is altered by Fire's need for the limelight. Fire imparts to the Dog more creativity, and he is less cynical than other members of his clan. This Dog will, on occasion, betray positively puppylike enthusiasm for new concepts and plans, and although he may always remain essentially hard to impress, he will doubtless be easy to entertain. What this Dog does need is a good example. He relates well to more stable types and persons older and wiser than himself, and will rely on a mentor or two in the course of his life to help him realize his leadership potential. In fact, Fire Dogs without a strong hand early on may become subject to addictions and self-destructive tendencies. They are more likely than other Dogs to seek to solve emotional problems with drugs or alcohol. Fire Dogs are not born aesthetes like the Metal Dog. The Fire Dog is courageous enough to wend his way through any amount of sticky politics. This is the original Comeback Kid. His idealism never deserts him even in the worst of circumstances.

The Earth Dog

The Earth element combines in this native to produce a personality capable of an almost eerie impartiality. The high idealism of the Dog is tempered here with an Earth nuts-and-bolts attitude to problem solving. Democratic notions form the backbone of this Dog and find him frequently following the principles of majority rule, as long as he can be certain it is the majority he follows. Earth makes the suspicious Dog even more secretive. He is unlikely to put his feelings on the line because he isn't altogether certain that others won't exploit them. He has a tendency to the cynicism of Dogs, which usually develops in old age in Dog natives. For an Earth type he is somewhat of an overachiever. Like his Metal-dominated counterpart, this Dog may make excessive demands on others because he is so demanding of himself. Earth's caution and carefulness direct this Dog to material concerns, but the Dog prompts him to share his worldly goods in charitable or philanthropic acts. He can be an excellent adviser because of his emotional distance coupled with an insight into what others do best. His guidance can be invaluable, his advice sound if not imaginative, and Earth gives him an innate wisdom which, in the Dog, translates to an inner purity of character. Absolute power will never corrupt this individual, nor is he likely to be self-indulgent. He can be a scrappy fighter, but you can be sure he will survive his battles. Whatever the outcome of any conflict, he is never overconfident in his triumphs or destroyed by his defeats. There is a part of him that loves the testing aspect that battle brings. Emotionally, he is rarely disappointed, except by disloyalty or unworthiness. But even then he is unlikely to desert others. An Earth Dog disillusioned will, however, be less inclined to personal issues and will throw himself into working solutions for the larger good of humanity.

The Five Types of Boar

The Metal Boar

Metal in this sign gives the Water-ruled Boar even more fortitude than the considerable amount naturally evident in the Boar native. He is also passionate. They only thing this Boar values more than his emotions is his comfort. Metal imparts an intensity to the Boar that could express itself in excess. This person is prone to grand appetites, work schedules, and an extreme lack of tact. He is very sociable and extroverted, if a bit prone to seeing the world through rose-colored glasses. He may underestimate his opponents and overestimate his allies because he likes to believe the best of all. The trusting qualities of the Boar influenced strongly by Metal may make him less able to tolerate well-meaning advice from others. He expects others to be open, honest, and forthright, just as he is. If they are not, he will turn a blind eye to the devious machinations of human interaction. Metal makes him more ambitious and stubborn than the rest of his kind. Coupled with the Boar's natural strength and imperviousness to pain, this person has immense endurance and personal fortitude, and is someone who never quits. If he should meet defeat head on, you can bet he won't be gracious or gentlemanly. Sportsmanlike behavior is not in his repertoire. Should he surround himself with those who can restrain his more self-indulgent tendencies, this Boar will excel in any area he chooses. The Boar makes Metal more optimistic and less inclined to self-defeating bouts of seclusion and sadness. The affectionate qualities of the Boar make it easier for Metal to express itself and less likely to shy away from exhibiting deep emotion. At its most positive, Metal makes the Boar more discriminating and intuitive than his innocent, trusting nature would normally dictate.

The Water Boar

Double Water in the Animal sign of the Boar creates a person who is immensely persuasive. Not only does he believe in miracles, he has no trouble getting others to believe in them as well. He is highly communicative, marked by earnestness and an enormous capacity for faith. The Boar's loyalty to others can turn positively religious in this configuration. All Boars are scrupulous and this Boar is particularly so. He is not afraid to meet others halfway or walk the extra mile should the situation call for assistance. Water plus Water in the sympathetic Boar makes him even more empathetic and kind. Yet as perceptive as he can be, he is marked by a Boar-like determination to refuse to see the very worst in situations and other people. He may be in far over his head before he realizes that he has been taken advantage of. Even then it will not matter once he has become committed to a course of action. Despite his childlike faith in the optimistic outcome of life, he is certain to indulge himself periodically in Boar-like appetite, which can be formidable. Because of his verbosity, he is capable of passionate declarations of love and earth-shaking devotion, which are followed by equally intense physical demonstration. Negatively aspected, Water is always inclined to self-indulgence. This is even more so in the Boar native. He needs to find constructive outlets for his highly physical nature in order not to get sidetracked from his goals. He also needs to channel his sensitivity in more discerning ways.

The Wood Boar

The Wood element makes the Boar more practical than he is ordinarily. He is also more aware of recognizing and acting upon his own self-interest. He is a superb fund-raiser, and is most likely devote his time to charity work, club activities, and group efforts. Above all else, this Boar lives to help and he can aid in expansive, organizational ways. Wood helps him be more subtle than he would ordinarily and more practical in translating his good-hearted impulses. Like all Boars, he places the utmost confidence in people, but Wood gives this native the ability to bring diverse personalities together in constructive and effective ways. The Wood Boar is the boss all workers dream of having. He is generous, fair, and open-minded—the kind who won't hesitate to throw a party or shell out a generous bonus for a job well done. You can be sure that his parties will be fun. He is truly appreciative of the work, effort, and talents of others and is dedicated to making his people shine. It is essential that he surround himself with individuals as scrupulous and dedicated as he himself is. Any Boar can quickly take on the character and personality of his associates and the Wood Boar is particularly adaptable. He dislikes confrontation (the Wood in him feels it takes too much time, the Boar resents disruption of the peace) and he tends to take the way of least resistance, no matter what the cost. Happy and positive, this Boar makes a splendid promoter of anything. His natural confidence and easygoing goodness can inspire more close-fisted types to finance his causes—which will always be practical ones, due to the influence of Wood. This element's expansiveness is tempered by the Boar's innate scrupulousness. People can trust him to put their money to good use, even though his entrepreneurial ventures may be ambitious. He will be sure to cover any pitfall in his path to the satisfaction of everyone.

The Fire Boar

Intrepid, courageous, and unfalteringly optimistic, the Fire Boar is the original Good-Time Charlie. He uses the energy of Fire to reach the greatest heights or to fall to the greatest depths. Either way, his way through life will be a spectacular lesson to others. Fire can overcome the natural passivity of Water and may result in a very pig-headed and obstinate individual. Like all Fire types, he can be an impressive leader capable of intense suffering and deprivation, as long as he is loved. The ambition of Fire is not necessarily for himself—he is not purely a power-seeker—the Fire Boar must be adored. Whatever his impulses, he is sure to follow them. He will not sit around thinking them over, either. For better or worse, this Boar is fearless and undaunted. Blessed with Fire's cheerfulness and the Boar's natural strength, he is loved and protected by the gods, possibly because they know in advance he will love and protect others in turn. He is dedicated to his loved ones and is motivated to accumulate wealth to provide for his family and friends. He thrives on his own ability to be generous in any and all circumstances and will see to it his loved ones live in the lap of luxury, even if he is too busy to enjoy it himself. He is at his best when responsible for a large group of people and is twice lucky when he can control his intensity and appetite for sensual experience.

The Earth Boar

Earth makes the Boar more sensible than he can be ordinarily and is likely to absorb Water's tendency to spread him out in all directions. Since Earth concerns itself with the tangible side of things, this Boar is likely to be highly productive and expend less of his considerable energy in the pursuit of pleasure. This animal has enormous endurance. The natural strength of the Boar combined with Earth makes him all but immune to the ravages of stress, and he is likely to be kind-hearted enough to haul not only his own share of the burdens of life, but that of quite a few others as well. The downside to the Earth Boar is that although he is invariably well-meaning, he may be a little less than refined, able to impart a whole new definition to the word *blunt*. The Earth Boar will have to worry about his weight throughout his life. He adores rich and hearty meals and may seriously weigh the risk of a heart attack against the demands of a low fat and cholesterol regime. Boars like the sensual side of life, and Earth people tend to portliness, particularly when they feel that their security has been adequately provided for. Regardless, the Earth Boar is possessed of extraordinary physical strength and stamina and could very well outlive the rest of us, no matter where he tips the scales. The Earth Boar may prove himself to be the lover you remember for the rest of your life. Both Earth and the Boar are extremely sensual, and a sexual encounter with this type is likely to leave everybody smiling. The Earth Boar is reliable and kind, but someone who avoids conflict if at all possible. He sometimes appears utterly implacable and even dull, but beware the Boar's temper. Few have ever seen an Earth Boar on the rampage, but those who have remember the scene for a very long time.

Chapter Four

POSITIVE AND NEGATIVE ASPECTS

All energy, or *ch'i*, is in constant movement. Huang Tzi, the Yellow Emperor, began his explanation of the Five Elements by stating that the Cosmos first divided itself into the duality of Yin and Yang, or negative and positive aspects. We have shown in preceding chapters that Yin and Yang represent certain nuances in how the Five Elements translate themselves: Positive fire is a conflagration, and Negative Fire is a cheerful bonfire. It will be easier to understand the elements in your chart if you understand the effect of Yin and Yang in more depth. The concept itself is simple. The world is in a constant state of change, alternating between action and rest. Yang represents the active force and Yin the passive force. Very few things in life are completely Yin or completely Yang, because most things are in transition, composed of a little of both elements. Think of a double A battery in which one terminal is positive, the other negative. In order to make any battery-operated toy or appliance work, it is important that both terminals be connected, moving energy in a functional way throughout the circuit.

The circuit itself makes complementary use of the natural antagonism of Yin and Yang, thus the meaning of the Taoist symbol of the whole. The positive terminal initiates the flow of energy and the negative terminal transforms that energy to produce the results for which the circuit was designed. It is easy to see from this simple illustration that what has a beginning has an end. The end begins a new cycle which, once it has run its course, circles back to the active impulse of the positive terminal. Together Yin and Yang produce energy and, in the case of the toy of appliance, the desired phenomenon.

Although Westerners may have a difficult time understanding this concept, it is quite prevalent in Western political, historic, and scientific thought. Hegel, the eighteenth-century philosopher, described the movement of human idea as a spiral, progressing from a given concept. Any concept produces the ability to entertain its opposite. Once its opposite has been fully described, both concepts will merge to produce a new idea, which combines elements of both. This will then produce its own opposite, and so on. Albert Einstein's theory of relativity translates this principle in another way, using the world of matter and the world of vibration. His theory states that vibration turns itself into matter, which turns itself into vibration, which is then manifest in matter. The twentieth-century historian Arnold Toynbee explained the course of human events as a constant cycle of challenge and response, the response itself becoming a challenge and eliciting another response.

But how do Yin and Yang cause movement in nature? Look around you and you will see that growth in nature almost always occurs in spirals. Galaxies expand and contract in a spiral. The hair on your head grows in spiral patterns, seashells are shaped in spirals, and the DNA molecule is a long spiral of genetic information. The spiral is the most natural shape found in our environment. Because the Taoists looked to nature for answers about the world, they applied these natural patterns of growth to change. The most concentrated force, the center of the spiral, they termed Yang; the most expansive force, the edge, they termed Yin. It is the nature of Yin growth to move from the center of a spiral to its outermost edge. The constant effects of Yang ensure that this happens gradually, in a circular movement, rather than in a straight line. The impulse to move from the outside into the center and form a concentration there (as in the motion of atoms or molecules) is described as a Yang process. The constant effect of Yin produces the spiral pathway.

Yin (Negative)

In general, Yin describes the direction of south, warm weather, strong taste, and odor. It is watery, more intuitive, more responsive and expansive than Yang. Yin growth patterns are vertical above ground and horizontal below ground. Think of a jungle, always expanding its perimeters, and you will have a good concept of the Yin principle. It houses giant growth, which in spots may exist in complete darkness. It shelters and nurtures a wealth of animal life under the forest umbrella. A tremendous amount of activity occurs beneath the surface of this umbrella—growth, rot, and decay followed by new growth are all essential to its system. We think of tropical forests as ancient, and indeed Yin reflects ancient principles of the rhythm of life. Put another way, Yin describes the feminine side of existence and experience. Fertility, birth, and rebirth are all Yin operatives. Yin moves slowly and requires a great deal of rest. Sleep and the night hours are ascribed to Yin, as are the subconscious and colder temperatures.

How does this apply to personalities? If your chart shows a domination of negative, or Yin, energy, you are likely to be taller and thinner than your Yang-dominated counterparts. Yin people have soft skin and hair and large, liquid eyes. They are not as intent upon expressing themselves and prefer mental to physical activity. They are concerned with all aspects of the psychological and the intuitive and are likely to be highly psychic. They feel deeply and do not like to stand out in a group. They are capable of working alone as long as their work is in the arts or sciences, and they are capable of putting great feeling into whatever they do. Yin types like to hear all sides of a problem before making a decision. They affect the world in subtle ways, infiltrating the opposition. They like peace and quiet and would rather flee than fight. In a confrontation, however, they wear down the opposition gradually, with little apparent effort on their part. Much remains beneath the surface in the Yin-dominated personality; in extreme instances, they are ruled almost entirely by subconscious motivations and hidden desires. They do not express themselves overtly, but they are nonetheless capable of wielding great influence.

Yang (Positive)

Where Yin expresses the "darker," expansive, subconscious side of life, Yang is like a sunny day. It is associated with northern, colder climates, and faint odors. This energy is assertive, concentrated, outwardly expressive and can, at times, be volcanic. Yang growth patterns are vertical below ground and horizontal above ground. Yang energy has been described as ascending and descending. If you think of a mountain peak, you will have a good visualization of the Yang principle.

As you progress further up the mountain, the air becomes colder. Mountain air is dry and mountain vegetation is shorter, hardier, and more geographically concentrated than the vegetation of our Yin example, the jungle, in which plants and trees must spread out in order to compete for survival. Mountains are composed of rock, compacted over time from soil and animal matter. Even rolling mountains have summits or peaks, a concentration of matter at the top. Mountains inspire aggressive physical activity and represent a challenge to the human imagination motivating us to "conquer" the summit, whereas the natural human response to a jungle is to uncover its secrets. Yang describes the masculine side of human assertion. It is active, forceful, and expects certain effects to follow specific causes. Yang moves quickly. Work and the day hours are ascribed to Yang, as are logic and deduction.

If your chart shows a preponderance of Yang, you will be happiest taking an active role in daily affairs. You are probably compact and muscular, capable of physical strength and endurance. Many Yang-dominated people are able to work tirelessly because of their ability to recharge themselves quickly. They do not require a great deal of thinking in order to make sense of the world and they enjoy the excitement of stress. Yang personalities are most comfortable when they can solve their problems through action. In arguments, they like to "bring things to a head," air their disagreements, and get on with life. They think of the world as a challenge and love taking risks of any kind. The information they gather will be used for a definite purpose. Organizations and corporations are Yang institutions. Yang people like to work with others in order to achieve their goals, and they would rather meet a situation head on than advance in a circuitous way. These are people who move forward. Time is a Yang concept, space is a Yin concept. Sometimes Yang people are not consistent in their use of energy. Although highly motivated to make their mark in the world, they may surprise observers by changing their course in midstream and taking an entirely new direction. Yang people like to get things done. They have a sixth sense about whether or not they can overcome an obstacle in their way. If they can't, they will stop on a dime and charge off in a completely new direction. Tremendously energetic, they can't abide slowing down or wasting time. These people fight to the death for what they believe in rather than negotiate or wait another day. Although passionate and emotional, Yang people are not prone to introspection. They like to know how things and people work in practical ways. They may change their minds, but it is easy to understand where they are coming from at any given moment. What you see is pretty much what you get. They are cheerful and optimistic, even when in the gravest danger, and they do not like to be caged or have their freedom limited in any way. On the negative side, they can be cruel and insensitive, insistent on forcing others to their will.

They must express themselves and their passionate natures through concrete action and can become destructive in their impatience for change.

Positive and Negative Stems

Once the basic concept of Yin and Yang is understood, it is easy to see how the Five Elements and the Twelve Animal signs or Earth Branches work. Each of the Five Elements has a positive and negative stem or, in other words, a Yin and Yang expression. Of the Twelve Animal signs, six are positive stem signs and six are negative stem signs. The Rat, Tiger, Dragon, Horse, Monkey, and Dog are positive signs. The Ox, Rabbit, Snake, Sheep, Rooster, and Boar are negative signs. When the Five Elements appear in the years of each Animal sign, they take on the positive or negative stem of the designated sign, as positive and negative stems alternate sequence throughout the cycle.

Each stem characterizes a different aspect of the positive or negative, depending upon in which Animal sign it resides. Although the character traits exhibited can be shared equally by men or women, it is easy to see why some signs are characterized as Yang and some as Yin.

The Yang or Positive Stem

The Rat begins each day. It also starts the astrological cycle. The Rat is associated with the masculine principles of initiation and protection. It describes a masculine way of commencing on a course of action.

The Tiger represents bravery, aggression, and the military, all ways in which the masculine force expands itself to bring the action of the Rat to fruition.

The Dragon expresses its masculinity in imagination and ideas. Its realm is male creativity and life force.

The Horse rules High Noon. Its month is the summer solstice, when the sun is at its most forceful. The Horse is associated with masculine desire, goals, and ambition.

The Monkey symbolizes male problem-solving abilities and versatility. It represents aggressive mental action and physical skill. It is an illustration of masculine behavior in the world of business or career.

The Dog, being a domestic animal, stands for the male influence in the home and represents guardianship, security, and an ability to fight for the rights of both property and weaker members of the household. It demonstrates the role of the active principal at work in the family.

The Yin or Negative Stem

The Ox is associated with fertility. Traditionally, it begins the Chinese Almanac, which starts with the harvest months. It gives itself to the earth and the treasures the Earth houses. It begins action in a Yin style, by being receptive.

The Rabbit has a long historical Chinese association with the Moon and expresses the feminine principle at work through the subconscious and healing. Chinese folklore gives the Rabbit possession of the elixir of life. It describes the Yin way of expanding its influence.

The Snake expresses the feminine world of ideas, imagination, and wisdom. It is also associated with mystery and intrigue.

The Sheep is the essence of the feminine and rules feminine behavior, as the Horse rules masculine behavior.

The Rooster embodies feminine ways of solving problems and reaching solutions. It is the "logic" of Yin as well as an expression of the endurance of Yin energy, which will wear down the opposition. It demonstrates feminine ways of behaving in business and career.

The Boar exemplifies the Yin principle at work in the home and expresses peace, rest, and completion, not only of the day, but also of the cycle itself.

As you can see, the positive and negative stems express themselves in dualities. The Rat, who is positive, and the Ox, who is negative, express themselves through building and planning. The Positive Tiger and the Negative Rabbit are evidence of Yin and Yang ways of growth and expansion. The Dragon, who is positive, and the Snake, who is negative, point toward the unknowable. The Positive Horse and the Negative Sheep exhibit male and female modes of behavior. The Positive Monkey and the Negative Rooster show how male and female behavior expresses itself in the external world of business, whereas the Positive Dog and the Negative Boar demonstrate the male and female principle in the home.

In order to discover how your predominant element or elements operate within your personality, you need to check your Birth Chart. Do positive or negative elements dominate? To what extent? Take this information, add it to your element, read the description, and apply it to the extent that the Dominating Element influences your birth chart. For instance, a person with three or more elements in Negative Water is a more extreme example of the personality described than one in which Negative Water figures once or twice.

Positive Metal

This person, while retaining all of the loner aspects of Metal, needs to express himself in active ways. He may be a restless wanderer, although he is more likely to move from place to place than from group to group. He will range far and wide, collecting impressions and storing information, but if he can't settle down, it will be difficult for him to assimilate his information concretely and give something back to the world. He is most likely a talker, although the subjects on which he chooses to discourse are more theoretical than practical. He has an inclination to be judgmental; Metal qualities of righteousness may exceed respect for others, and he may be self-righteous in his approach to the world. Although he understands other people, he is not personal in his approach to human affairs. He is able to inspire others to excel and strive for the best through his words and action. He may drive himself to accumulate money and material goods in order to maintain his independence. He is enterprising and businesslike, courageous in the face of danger, and entrepreneurial by nature. He wants to live up to his own lofty expectations of proper human behavior in the world. In extreme cases, he will do well to think before he speaks, otherwise he will not achieve the results he desires. Enraged, he can electrocute his opposition without a moment's thought.

Negative Metal

The Negative Metal person is a radio antenna to the world around him. He is happy to spend his life in one place because he can find a store of information and interest in the most microscopic detail. He, like his dominant Water element brother, is almost psychic in the accuracy of his impressions. But whereas Water personalities are more concerned with other people and their motivations, the Negative Metal person is inclined to focus his attention on trends in human affairs. He thinks and feels deeply, but he may be subject to mood swings dictated to him by his passionate romantic nature. He has immense powers of concentration and does not like it when others try to spur him on to courses of action. He probably has a difficult time expressing himself. Although he is full of new ideas and inventions, he is often unable to talk about them. Others feel his magnetic energy, no matter how his moods are affecting him. He has a great ability to heal and his touch is profound. He is interested in trying to popularize new and untried theories if he feels they are accurate in their application. He may be quite shy and he is certainly not one to take risks. He needs to learn to be more decisive. If anything, he is too receptive to the vacillating electrical impulses around him. He is not skilled in social interaction and may appear quite odd, but he can adapt to a contemplative, solitary life and is probably adept at writing or the arts. He is creative, drawing on the world around him for inspiration. Whereas the Positive Metal person may have too many sharp edges to be truly understood by others, the Negative Metal person may be difficult to get along with in one-on-one situations. Still, he is able to exist happily in situations that most others would find completely untenable.

Positive Water

This person, like the Positive Metal individual, undoubtedly leads a nomadic existence. But here, he is in search of new people and experiences rather than absolutes. He has a multitude of associations and personal contacts and can pass through all levels of society with no problem, but he may be far too expansive to accomplish his goals and may spread himself too thin. Although extremely active, he can end up frenetically repeating the same chore over and over again. Intellectually, he could be dilettantish in his superficial understanding of ideas and concepts, because he seems unable to take the time to delve more deeply. He is a great talker, witty, bright, and amiable, and he can fool less discerning souls. He is also adventurous, seeking new sensations and feelings and, in the more extreme examples, is never at home. Obstacles may divert him, but if there are elements in the chart to mitigate this, he will be able to wear down his opposition unrelentingly. He is most happy when he is active and outgoing. Although he may choose an intellectual life, he wants to make a lasting contribution to his discipline. He influences others emotionally, but may not stick around to make the best use of the results. At the very worst, the torrential force of his personality can tear others up by the roots. He would do well to treat others and himself gently. If he can manage this, he is capable of great sympathy and understanding.

Negative Water

The Negative Water person, although he may be secretive and enigmatic, is very much the intellectual. His secrecy results from a desire for privacy and an innate shyness rather than from any desire to engage in double-dealing, although his actions may be misinterpreted by others. This person is the ultimate example of still waters running deep, although at his most negative he could be a stagnant pond. An extreme personality of this type has difficulty getting himself to move at all, both physically and mentally. But most likely, this individual is more of the reflecting pool variety, able to mirror people and situations around him with accuracy and grace. The Negative Water person is charming and diplomatic in his dealings with others. He intuitively understands complicated motives and scenarios. Although he may not speak a great deal, his comments are certain to reflect wisdom and understanding. He is most at home in an environment that is soothing and beautiful, from which he can observe the strenuous activity of human drama and draw his own conclusions. He sometimes seems more wise than he actually is, although by the time he has reached maturity he has paid close attention to the patterns and intricacies of life and has well-perceived views about what he has experienced. He does not like to rush into action. He is cautious and reserved in all matters, from his relationships with others to his business activity. And although he relishes his time alone he is gracious to those who seek his advice.

If he can overcome early disappointments, which he feels deeply and intensely, and put his emotions into perspective, he could well achieve sage status during his lifetime. He does not respond well to those who try to pressure him into doing what they think he should do. He will wait, gather his strength, and act. He is almost as patient as the Earth signs, but his is a communicative, emotional element. He observes and expresses himself in an insightful running commentary on events and social sitations. He never stridently incites others to right wrongs like the Positive Metal individual. He may be lazy and narrow-minded if his environment does not meet his aesthetic qualifications, and he has a remarkable ability to take care of himself when the need arises.

Positive Fire

Fire is the element that represents reason, expressiveness, good manners and, oddly enough, social graces. It shows up injustice for what it is and attempts to effect change. Positive Fire people try to change things for the better whether others around them want it or not. Naturally, in the beginning, Fire people believe this to be for the good of everyone. But Fire people can quickly get swept away by enthusiasm and they tend to tyrannize those weaker than themselves. This tyranny can escalate to cruelty. Badly aspected, Positive Fire people can be bossy, loud, and agressive, both physically and verbally. The cabdriver who gets out of his cab to start a fight in the middle of an intersection is most likely a Positive Fire personality. They can also get so caught up in the drama of fighting that they leave carnage in their wake. Because they have a tremendous amount of energy available, they don't always know when to stop. What's worse, they have a genuine ability to get others as enraged as they are themselves—it's that Fire leadership and enthusiasm at work influencing whatever their touch. Positive Fire types can be excellent at blazing trails and risking their necks to prove new ideas and theories, but they can be a little overwhelming when they are forced into a boring environment with nothing to do. If they can channel some of their energy internally, spark the enthusiasm of others to try new things, and learn to let off steam in productive ways, Positive Fire people can be among the most insightful of any of the Five Elements. What's more, they get things done. When they are not extreme, they have the ability to convince others that even the most arduous of tasks is a great adventure. If controlled, their criticism is sensible and fair. But they must learn when to stop or their criticism can be picky and relentless. Even though they mean well, others tend to turn them off because their lack of perspective makes them judge others harshly without sympathy or understanding.

Negative Fire

If Positive Fire personalities run the risk of demolishing the egos of those around them, Negative Fire personalities are in even more danger—of combusting internally. These people need to learn to let their feelings out. Physical activity can help them to vent their emotions and frustrations in constructive ways, and sort out the background noise from the valid crusading. Negative Fire people can be particularly adept at internalizing their anger. This can become so extreme as to render them unable to fight for themselves, a sorry situation for a Fire individual. They can still attract and inspire followers and hangers-on, but their leadership ability will be diverted toward sensationalism. Negative Fire people deprived of direction or an outlet for expression may give off dangerous signals indeed. In fact, many of them seem to be accidents about to happen. The Fire quality of ambition can be oddly translated in this instance into a complete lack of motivation about anything. An extreme Negative Fire personality may blow hot and cold. He may have moments of intense destructiveness that alternate with periods of great lethargy. He may ignore others and become selfishly involved with his own needs and problems. A Fire person must be around others to be truly happy, but this person may find others avoiding him. He reacts by trying to dominate those left in his circle with his creativity and impulsiveness. The Negative Fire person is receptive to new ideas, but he may have problems implementing them. In this case, he would do well to become more outspoken, because all those pent-up feelings have a negative effect on this person's internal health. He is prone to internalizing stress in his organs and is an excellent candidate for stomach disorders. This is one person who might find aggressiveness training helpful. He may be a gossip and talk about others behind their backs because he has such a difficult time with confrontation. If this person can learn to let go (odd advice for a Fire personality), however, he can be fair in his appraisement of others and considerate in his dealings, capable of diplomacy and humor.

Positive Wood

A person with a medium amount of Wood is well-balanced and flexible, able to incorporate the ideas and beliefs of others into his own value system. He is not put off by opposition, but is able to bend with the winds of circumstance and still be true to himself. A person with an overabundance of wood is impervious to shifts in the climate around him, but may be so inflexible about larger issues that he could very well become uprooted. We have already seen that Wood-elemental people value their ethics almost as much as they value far-reaching plans and new ideas, which they like to implement into workable systems. This person looks for far-reaching results, but he may be less patient than a person whose Wood element is more balanced. He may tend to force people into preconceived notions of what he believes is workable and not allow others enough freedom to act independently of his organizational view. Should he proceed along this course, he will find himself deprived of what he values most—new ideas and concepts. He may be overconfident and hasty in his desire to reach new goals, although he is still able to convince others to back his ventures. In his desire for growth, he may spread himself too thin, or become so detail oriented that he slows down the expansion and growth he needs so desperately to survive. He may be overly generous, to his own detriment, always expecting to have unlimited supplies of money and resources, or his schemes may become so grandiose that they are no longer practical. Although compassionate and sympathetic to the needs of others, this person may sacrifice the organization he has worked so hard to build for the sake of doing good deeds, disregarding the fact that people need to do things for themselves. The ability to stick to a course of action once decided upon despite all adversity may become evident in extreme examples of the Positive Wood-dominated personality. Positive Wood people may have trouble letting go should their plans meet with opposition. And they may push their employees and plans past any hope of a realistic solution. Although blessed with native resilience, this person finds it difficult to transform his energy and redirect it if his plans reach an impasse. He needs to learn to give and take. Compromise is a Wood blessing and he should surround himself with advisers whose opinion he respects. If he can remain open and adaptable despite the fact that his wishes and intentions are being thwarted, he can forestall the unfortunate events that may occur as a result of his active, workaholic nature.

Negative Wood

A person with a preponderance of Negative Wood would do well not to cave into the wishes of others in order to keep the peace. Although he has a great fund of new ideas bubbling up under the surface, he may not be able to actualize them, either due to unfavorable circumstances or to his own inability to verbalize his concepts adequately. Still, people trust him and his ideas, and support his concepts. The person with a preponderance of Negative Wood may lack the self-confidence that characterizes his positive brother. Being Wood dominated, such persons are likely to be put in administrative or executive positions, but they may dissipate this authority by listening to the advice and counsel of others to such an extent that they appear indecisive or noncommittal. The Negative Wood personality can spread itself and its resources much too thin. It is natural to the Wood personality to expand in order to solve problems, and this trait is only exacerbated by the Yin influence. Others may look to him for leadership, but will find themselves frustrated when he changes his mind and alters his decisions to conform with newer concepts and ways of doing things. This person can abandon whole systems of operation with little notice. He does have the Wood-based understanding of others, and is able to smooth things out temporarily. But he must understand that it is his own energy, indecisiveness, and a tendency to overexpansion that are at the base of many of the trials and upheavals he faces in life. The Negative Wood personality is always found in the public arena—they are the people who "have greatness thrust upon them." Yet, because he is Yin-based, he will always long for more private kinds of contact. Rather than being seen as an authority, this individual wants to exert subtler forms of influence, playing the quiet diplomat and working behind the scenes.

Positive Earth

Earth people are practical and giving, but the Positive Earth personality may be almost too concerned with the needs of others. He resembles a Water-dominated personality in his sincerity and concern for those less fortunate. Earth people have a well-deserved reputation for being adept with money and financial investments of all kinds, but a Positive Earth type may dissipate his resources through an overly generous attitude and jeopardize the security of which he is so fond. Although honest and loyal, he is also very outgoing and not as generally modest as Earth might indicate. The

Positive Earth personality is blunt to the point of cruelty at times, although never deliberately so. This type of Earth personality is not so methodical and is prone to jump to conclusions with both feet. He can be more impatient than the character of Earth types would lead one to believe. Here, Earth's natural slowness may express itself in procrastination; he tends to dissipate his energies and intelligence by acting before he thinks. Dominated by Yang energy, the Earth person may go too fast and be too expressive for his own good. Through the sheer strength of his personality, he may try to impose his own natural conservatism on others, and be somewhat shortsighted. Nonetheless, he will stick by you until the bitter end and will never sit in judgment on those he cares for. The task for him is in learning to integrate the systematic approach of Earth with the Positive need to act. Otherwise, he can prove to be his own worst enemy and fail to utilize his considerable talents and resources.

Negative Earth

These people have an innate need to build for the future because it represents security in an uncertain, ever-changing world. They are obsessed with taking care of themselves and those they love, and worry constantly about their safety. The impulse of Earth energy is to nurture and sustain life, but always on their own terms. To be truly successful in their relationships, they need to give freely, with no strings attached. These people can be so protective they fail to recognize the advantages of risk taking over the predictable. Yin with Earth can make these individuals highly manipulative and subversive in the process of getting where they want to go. They are best behind the scenes, though, for they have a difficult time expressing themselves and their goals. This type can be secretive because he is so concerned with protecting himself and all the possessions he has acquired to date. They can be very introspective, which is uncharacteristic of the Earth dominated. Again, their introspection is based on concern for survival and security. In extreme cases, this need can reach paranoic proportions and paralyze their ability to act effectively. Negative Earth types can find themselves embroiled in all sorts of intrigues, which can be detrimental, because Earth itself is usually happiest when it can be straightforward. Still, the Negative Earth type operates more effectively in theoretical modes and is not so relentlessly practical. If they can learn to balance their considerable intuitions and somewhat obsessive tendencies with practical intelligence and application, it will do much to overcome their subversive side and relax them in the long run.

Chapter Five

COMPATIBILITY AMONG THE FIVE ELEMENTS

As we have seen in earlier chapters, the elements operate in a never-ending cycle of creation and destruction, followed by creation once again. Naturally then, as the elements move through their creative and destructive cycles, they express themselves in relationship to each other. So, too, do people dominated by those elements. Therefore, the elemental relationships must be considered in the interpretation of individual charts, as they do, in fact, have some bearing on the way individuals interact.

The creative cycle, beginning with Metal, moves from Metal to Water, Water to Wood, Wood to Fire, Fire to Earth, and Earth to Metal. Each element in this sequence derives energy from the element preceding it and conducts energy through the cycle. It is easy to see that, in this relationship, conducive elements are highly compatible. There is an instant recognition and sympathy for others in the cycle and all will help and nurture each other.

The destructive cycle, beginning with Metal, moves to Wood, Earth, Water, Fire, and back to Metal. These elements cause negative effects on each other when the direction of energy proceeds in that order. The tendency here is to cancel each other out.

When it comes to the question of personality compatibility among the elements, Chinese sages recommend making friends and associates whose dominant element substitutes for a deficient element or elements in one's own chart. Obviously, however, one must exercise caution in dealing with people whose dominant element is followed by one's own in the destructive cycle. Similarly, it is easy to ride roughshod over the person whose dominant element is next in line from your own. Deep understanding and discipline must be exercised in such a relationship. There may not be a great deal of innate understanding of why the individual behaves as he does. In conflicted elemental relationships, another's behavior and motivation may appear foreign and difficult to understand.

As to relationships with other elements, the following charts may prove helpful.

The following table illustrates each dominant element, followed by those elements with which there are the most compatible relationships, the most incompatible relationships, and those that may be somewhat conflicted, but in which there is a possibility of harmony.

TABLE 5-1:
ADVANTAGEOUS/DISADVANTAGEOUS/ AND RECONCILABLE ELEMENTAL RELATIONSHIPS

HIGHLY ADVANTAGEOUS:

DOMINANT ELEMENT	COMPATIBLE ELEMENTS
Metal	Water, Wood
Fire	Wood, Metal
Water	Fire, Wood
Earth	Water, Metal
Wood	Earth, Water

HIGHLY DISADVANTAGEOUS:

DOMINANT ELEMENT	INCOMPATIBLE ELEMENTS
Metal	Fire
Fire	Water
Water	Earth
Wood	Metal
Earth	Wood

RECONCILABLE DIFFERENCES:

DOMINANT ELEMENT	POSSIBLY COMPATIBLE ELEMENT
Metal	Earth
Fire	Earth
Water	Metal
Earth	Fire
Wood	Fire

SYMPATHETIC:

DOMINANT ELEMENT	SYMPATHETIC ELEMENT
Metal	Metal
Fire	Fire
Water	Water
Earth	Earth
Wood	Wood

Let's see how these relationships of element-dominated personalities interact more specifically, based on our knowledge of the Five Element personalities. Note that nowhere in Table One is it stated that any elemental relationship is necessarily incompatible or hopelessly conflicted. We have already seen that the Five Elements are interrelated and co-dependent; each relationship is therefore important, regardless of its nature.

A word of caution: In any astrological analysis or system of personality interpretation, one must always take into consideration the personalities themselves, and never sacrifice preferences of the individual to the system. Always remember that such systems were meant to be used for guidance, not put forth as irrefutable evidence of destiny. As mentioned earlier, the Chinese Masters recommended that any person augment his or her chart with elements missing from the birth chart, or surround himself with friends and associates in whom the missing elements predominate. As you read over the following material, keep in mind that whenever the possibility for conflict exists, it is equally possible for the conflicted elements to complement one another, providing that the individuals involved make the effort to achieve the necessary understanding and harmony.

The Metal/Water Relationship

Both these individuals are guided by strong intuitions and are governed by feelings, rather than facts. Metal is, however, directed inward, whereas Water expands and travels outward. Water here has much to teach Metal about social interaction and the ability to influence others in subtle ways, and can do a great deal to overcome Metal's natural tendency to take the road less traveled. For example, Water people enable Metal people to better communicate their emotions and help them to be more flexible in their dealings with the world at large. The Water person also helps Metal through his or her moodier turns and, in inimitable water style, subliminally helps to convince stubborn Metal to actually give up on some of those hopeless crusades and lost causes. In turn, the Metal-dominated person in this relationship helps the Water personality strengthen his or her inner convictions and not be so easily influenced by others. Metal teaches Water to play their hunches and not to take their intuitions so much for granted, and shows Water how to be less volatile and more patient with those whose attitudes are not as flexible as their own. The Metal type strives to protect the Water type in a relationship of this kind, and Water responds well to Metal's regenerative powers. Metal imparts a great deal of stability and loyalty to Water in this relationship, and helps the Water type to depersonalize a bit and gain the larger perspective when Water threatens to founder in a pool of his own emotions.

The Metal/Wood Relationship

Both of these types are used to having their own way, and Metal will probably dominate here. This pairing can be somewhat less advantageous to Wood than to Metal because of Metal's tendency to solitude. His need to go it alone will frustrate that highly social team player lurking just beneath the bark of any Wood personality. Still, Wood's cooperative nature undoubtedly lets Metal do pretty much as he wants, even to the suppression of his own needs and desires. Yet, Metal trusts Wood implicitly and both elements operate according to a highly developed code of ethics. Wood can teach Metal a great deal about social interaction and may even convince him on the merits of the occasional team effort. Both types are highly responsible, and Wood can doubtless find a way to put Metal's vision into practical application. But neither type is particularily self-effacing, and there will doubtless be some conflict as to just how things are to be done. Metal will be impatient with Wood's painstaking attention to detail and his logical, rather than inspirational, approach to life. Although Metal prefers to fight the good fight alone, Wood finds such isolation alien to his nature, preferring to organize and administrate others. In this relationship, it is up to Metal to allow himself to be led from time to time, trusting in Wood's good sense and practicality. If he does, all will go smoothly. Metal can teach Wood much about the merits of one-on-one relationships, and in his turn can learn from Wood the advantages of a wide social and professional network.

The Fire/Wood Relationship

Fire and Wood are natural allies. The long-term planning of Wood can be put to good use here, because he gives Fire solid ways and means to promote all those causes and crusades. Wood imparts stability to the wealth of Fire's enthusiasms and teaches Fire to be more ethically discriminating and not quite so enchanted with the virtues of anything new. In turn, Fire enables Wood to achieve his goals more quickly. Both types are outer-directed and are doubtless sympathetic to the other's aspirations. Wood helps Fire think more of the long term and finish what he starts, and is stimulated by Fire's curiosity and progressiveness. Both love experiments and new ideas, and neither, thankfully, minds an occasional fit of temper or explosive outburst. Inspirational Fire helps Wood to commit himself and there is less danger of Wood's spreading out in all directions, or becoming overly concerned with the opinions of others. Wood, in turn, is protective of Fire in this context. Fire imparts drama, passion, and serves to personalize Wood's dealings with others. He is adept at verbalizing and popularizing Wood's well-considered plans. Both are optimistic, and can accomplish much. Wood thrives on Fire's intensity and Fire can get Wood to laugh at himself and see things in a less serious light.

The Fire/Metal Relationship

At best, this is a highly competitive situation and one in which egos will doubtless collide from time to time. Dramatic Fire will appear to dominate in the outward sense here, but keep one eye open—Metal can fool you. Both are highly idealistic, but Fire tends to be more personally ambitious, whereas Metal crusades for what he believes in. Both are fond of new and outrageous ideas and trends, and this pair may be found on the very cutting edge of the avant-garde. Both these types are born rule breakers. Fire can and will publicize Metal inspirations and discoveries in ways that less intellectual types can readily absorb—providing he understands that Metal has little or no interest in knocking Fire out of his place in the limelight. Fire teaches Metal a certain finesse, and can do much to smooth off some of Metal's rougher edges. Metal in his turn teaches Fire to stick to a course of action, even when the going gets tough. The real saving grace in this situation is that both types are gifted with a great sense of humor, which can be relied upon to diffuse at least some of their difficulties. If Metal can withstand the heat of Fire's temper, and if Fire can learn the necessary patience with Metal moodiness and solitude, this can be a highly complementary and stimulating situation.

The Water/Fire Relationship

It may be hard for these two to understand one another, yet both types are blessed with formidable communication skills. Still, Fire tends to oratory and inspiration of groups, whereas Water excells at one-on-one conversation and empathy. Water can control Fire in this relationship, providing that he does not overreact to Fire's excessiveness and theatricality. Fire in turn can serve to inspire Water. Both like new ideas and people, and are adept at personal relationships. Fire provides the social graces and finesse, and Water provides the understanding. Still, both types have something to learn in the areas of endurance and energy maintenance. The danger here is in simply spreading out in all directions, or getting involved in frenetic, repetitive activity. In this combination, more than any other, there is the possibility of making the same mistakes over and over. If monitored, however, Water can teach Fire some subtlety, and how to cope with a variety of situations and societies, somewhat relieving Fire's continual need to be first in everything. Fire can relinquish some of its natural jealousy in this relationship, and Water can respond favorably to Fire's natural optimism and enthusiasm.

The Water/Wood Relationship

This is an excellent combination, marked by growth, understanding, and expansion. Water channels Wood's compassion into those areas where it does the most good, whereas Wood in turn gives Water direction and purpose. Water does much to personalize and attune Wood to individual needs and motivations, because of its innate understanding of the workings of the psyche. Wood teaches Water the best and most practical ways of utilizing its information and intuitions, and of putting those ideas to work in practical ways. Water does a great deal to complement and improve upon Wood's communication skills and, in some instances, can truly serve as the power behind the throne, to the delight and satisfaction of everyone involved. Water respects Wood's sincerity and ethical sense, and Wood admires Water's empathy and understanding. Wood can motivate Water, and Water strives to live up to Wood's expectations and ideals. Wood's enthusiasm is contagious to moodier Water types, and Water can serve to soften the administrative side of Wood's nature by imbuing it with a sense of the personal.

The Earth/Water Relationship

Earth is likely to try to dominate in this context, but will have to proceed carefully, because Water always tries to slip from its grasp. Earth imparts the natural common sense and stability that Water lacks, but both have to guard against emotionalism. If these two can't learn to forgive and forget, there could be a muddy mess indeed. Water sustains Earth emotionally and brings to it new ideas and possibilities for growth in nonconfrontational ways. This is a highly intellectual combination that does well to talk things out. Earth can heal and regenerate Water, and Water appreciates Earth's natural wisdom. But if Earth turns stubborn and unyielding, Water is just as likely to run off in twelve different directions. Earth strives to protect Water in this combination, and Water wants to sustain Earth. These two types can make an excellent team, particularly when Earth oversees the more practical side (i.e., food, shelter, and money), and Water oversees the emotional needs of the relationship. Water serves to make Earth more flexible and versatile, whereas Earth provides Water with security and direction. Earth works tirelessly to correctly analyze and assimilate all the data and information that Water so tirelessly supplies, and mitigates Water's tendency to exaggerate.

The Earth/Metal Relationship

This is an excellent combination in which both parties can thrive. Earth serves to ground Metal and impart a practicality to Metal's loftier ideals and crusades, and Metal stimulates Earth and enables him to take more chances. Here, Earth serves to condense and crystallize Metal's inner convictions and hunches into realized plans. Earth can serve as Metal's sounding board, adviser, and reality check. Both are bound to respect and admire the other's endurance. Earth serves to revitalize Metal and can even breathe a certain amount of life and inspiration into the lost causes that Metal can become involved in. There is mutual passion here—physical on the one hand and intellectual on the other. Metal is likely to be patient with Earth's cautious and slow-moving ways, and in fact feels more comfortable knowing that someone is capable of pacing him. Regardless of the individual missions involved, both types are exceedingly loyal and are well aware that they are in this relationship for the long haul. Minor obstacles will be met by each of them with equal aplomb and there are likely to be few temper tantrums or histrionic scenes in this context. Metal's deep ambition is likely to be mitigated by Earth's concern for the needs of the less fortunate, whereas Metal can inspire Earth to be more exciting. And both are likely to make allowances for the other's natural stubbornness. The relationship is likely to be financially as well as emotionally secure. Each of these types has highly developed instincts for accumulation and financial gain, and both use their wealth and influence to do good in the world.

The Wood/Earth Relationship

Wood is likely to dominate in this situation, and it must be careful in its dealings with Earth, because Wood is the only element that can actually deplete Earth resources. Here Wood strives to be progressive and modern, whereas Earth clings to the tried and true. If not balanced, Wood can easily take advantage of Earth, exploiting his loyalty and hardworking ways to achieve Wood's own ends. Wood expansiveness is likely to exasperate Earth and worry him to no end, while Wood is likely to grow impatient and bored with Earth's more cautious approach. The Wood tendency to fits of temper may keep the Earth personality working overtime to mend fences and return things to the status quo. Nonetheless, Earth can channel Wood energy in truly constructive ways, and Wood serves to expand Earth's social and professional network. Both elements are detail oriented, and there are times when Wood will do well to heed Earth's practical and careful advice. Earth appreciates Wood's practicality, if not the grandiosity of his schemes and plans. But perhaps the greatest danger here is that both have a difficult time expressing their feelings. If they can overcome that hurdle, their relationship will doubtless proceed with greater ease.

The Wood/Water Relationship

This is a fortunate combination—both types are fond of expansion and are attracted to new ideas, people, and situations, and face the world with a decidedly futuristic view. Water provides Wood with a strong, unconfined, emotional base, and Wood harnesses and directs Water's energy in constructive ways. Water smooths the way for Wood— Wood can "float" on Water, and will not be so inclined to dissipate its energies in detail work or failed communication. In fact, Wood appreciates the fact that Water wants to do all the talking for the two of them. Prolonged association enables Wood to improve and truly personalize his communications on a variety of levels. Water meets Wood's fits of temper with implacable calm and genuine humor. Water helps Wood to understand the needs of the individual and to keep a more flexible administrative attitude. Wood, after all, has to allow Water personal freedom (Water doubtless charms him into it, anyway), and in the process of relinquishing some control, Wood learns the value of going with the tide from time to time. Here Water gives Wood more intellect and emotion, and Wood imparts to Water an objective, fair-minded attitude.

The Metal/Metal Relationship

Metal types understand each other implicitly. Although their ideas and views may seem to be plugged into entirely different realities, this is a naturally empathetic team who will doubtless be able to unite for the purpose of achieving mutual goals or fighting for common causes. Although there is the potential for some conflict when two Metal types come together, generally these two are able to accept and adapt to one another's vision of the universe in true intellectual style—without an excess of emotion or ego getting in the way. Though Metal personalities are used to going it alone, they will doubtless be delighted at the prospect of discovering a kindred spirit or two on the path, and will be equally relieved that they won't have to constantly explain themselves to another Metal type. Metal/Metal relationships are usually of long duration. Even if these two don't appear to be especially close, there is always a symbiotic quality to this combination, and when they combine their farsighted Metal vision and join forces, they can be an awesome team.

The Fire/Fire Relationship

Watching this pair in action can be a truly mesmerizing, even exhausting, experience. They doubtless capture the imagination of others with their flair for drama, aura of excitement, and sophisticated conversation. The more destructive qualities of Fire tend to be mitigated somewhat in this context. Each understands the other's needs and each strives to protect the other from undue recklessness and harm. Yet even their protective urges are executed in inimitable Fire style, with none of those stuffy, cautious, or cloying conditions that the Fire personality finds so deeply offensive. These two trust each other and bring out the best in one another. They are able to compete for the fun of it, and thrive on one another's challenges. Their combined optimism and enthusiasm for life is unbeatable and will prove positively inspiring to all who come in contact with them. Here, Fire energy is more progressive and constructive and not so prone to those spectacular highs and lows that characterize the Fire personality alone. They accomplish and effect any necessary changes by challenging one another. Their love is characterized by a sustained passion that few other combinations can muster, and they find a childlike astonishment in their continual discovery of one another.

The Water/Water Relationship

Water combinations are one of two types: rushing streams that move side by side, or deep and reflecting pools. Water people have such a deep psychic affinity for each other that it appears, quite correctly, that there is nothing in heaven or on earth that can come between them. Whether these two are rushing off in all directions or reflecting the world back to itself, this relationship is always marked by the same distinct ability to understand and adapt to each other's moods and emotions. The Water/Water combination exerts a calming influence on its partners, and neither is prone to hypersensitivity and nervous disorders. Their natural resonance insulates them from a great many upsets and discords. The Water type can use its considerable intuitive powers to exploit others, and although this couple always has its own best interests at heart, Water's tendency to be self-serving is mitigated by the partner's gentle influence. Also, Water is not so passive or easily influenced in this combination, and spends it energy in nurturing, rather than dissipating itself in emotional excess.

The Wood/Wood Relationship

The Wood/Wood combination is a dynamic one. Both these people are go-getters and they will combine forces to get what they want from the world. They are constantly expanding their spheres of interest and social circles. These people take great delight in organizing and making lists for each other, and hold in highest esteem the other's ethical codes and decisions. They work unflaggingly to reach a common goal and plan down to the smallest detail before embarking on a course of action. They surround themselves with creative, quick-thinking types, who in turn serve to stimulate and inspire the Wood/Wood pair. The Wood/Wood combination is likely to be involved in everything from community work to politics, and their expansive approach to life will see them running a positively awesome network of home, business, social life, and neighborhood with unflagging good humor and tireless energy. There won't be any arguments in this household about late working hours or the joint checking account. Each is concerned with long-range goals and is only too happy to share his or her grandiose visions of the future with a like-minded partner. They place the utmost faith and confidence in one another, and there is little personal insecurity regarding their true place in their partner's scheme of things. Of course, there might also be very little conversation about it either, but Wood is rarely comfortable in heart-to-heart discussions, and this is one situation where taking each other more or less for granted can be quite comfortable for everyone concerned. Should either of them become overextended, the other is sure to come to the rescue, taking up the slack and reorganizing affairs so things can return to an even keel. Nonetheless, this relationship is marked by patience and tolerance, even in fits of temper, and can be seen as one of the truest examples of real give and take.

The Earth/Earth Relationship

Earth people supply each other with all the necessities and comforts of life—good food, a fine home, and long-term security, together with a nearly inexhaustible well of love and understanding. They wait on one another hand and foot and take great delight in shoring up that bank balance together. Their passionate natures help them through those sticky patches that can crop up when one or the other of them digs in and refuses to change, but since neither one is prone to an overabundance of adventurous plans, those kinds of problems are likely to be few and far between. Theirs will be the slow and methodical courtship and might seem just the teensiest bit dull to the uninitiated outsider. But rest assured this is a passionate twosome, whether or not they choose to show that to the world at large. They exert a healing influence on one another, and will, over time, become so self-sufficient that they can become quite isolated from the broader social network. The original Mom and Pop operation was undoubtedly the brainchild of an Earth couple, and they will build and sacrifice for years on end to make such a dream come true. This is one of the most secure combinations possible, and strangely, such a combination may do much to temper Earth's fear of change. Having the secure emotional base that an Earth partner provides enables these personalities to view the world with somewhat less trepidation and reserve, and although they may never belong to the avant-garde, they may be more flexible in combination than the Earth type alone.

Thus far, we have examined elemental compatability in its most constructive, or creative, terms. As you can see in Table One, some elements are naturally sympathetic and complementary, whereas other combinations are not. Certainly it can be seen, for example, that a potential for conflict exists in the Wood/Metal Relationship, because this combination is part of the destructive cycle. (Metal destroys Wood.) This does not mean that such relationships cannot succeed, only that greater concessions and compromises will be necessary to make them work.

Yet everyone encounters conflict with other personalities, sometimes without explanation of why those conflicts occur. Should you find yourself in one of those seemingly impossible, no-win situations (a boss/employee relationship, for example), we include the following analyses of elemental relationships in the destructive cycle. Remember as you refer to them, however, that no matter what the destructive potential in an elemental combination, each element is uniquely equipped to protect itself against the possibilities of destruction. Once aware of the operative factors, the individual can always insure himself against undue exploitation and unhappiness in any situation and recognize such situations as containing true potential for growth and development.

Metal/Fire

Fire, out of all the elements, has the ability to transform Metal into a molten mess. Central to the conflict here is Metal's tendency to impose his will on Fire—an exercise in futility. Stubbornness and conviction do not succeed against Fire's destructive side. Metal's ideological side will perish when pitted against the force of Fire's ego, and Fire can exploit Metal's ideas as his own, unless Metal is careful to remember not to retreat into solitude. The key to Metal's survival in a destructive situation of this kind is simply to endure. Fire energy, although impressive, always shows itself in fits and starts. Metal, with its great strength, can outlast the drama—providing he doesn't get burned.

Fire/Water

In this combination, Fire can be extinguished by the energies of Water. While Fire is a grandstander, Water's influence is always subtler and, hence, more pervasive. Water, too, has more natural empathy and greater understanding of any opposition, and can defeat Fire's optimism and enthusiasm through emotionalism. In this case, Fire must learn to survive by resisting its urge to confront. Water is always able to undermine Fire's dramatics through grass-roots support and the ability to win others over through pure emotionalism. If Fire can learn not to place his ego first and not to allow himself to be baited into precarious positions, he can survive.

Water/Earth

In a destructive combination, Earth may suffocate Water's need to spread out and expand. In the name of Water's own good, Earth will try to restrict Water in any number of ways, and may threaten to absorb Water's identity altogether into itself, unless Water can learn to maintain some objectivity. Nonetheless the communicative powers of Water can rally any number of allies to itself and should depend upon this quality in a destructive situation with the Earth personality. Water's subtle powers of influence and psychic gifts are ineffective against Earth's endurance and stubbornness. The best course of action here is simply to put another personality into the situation. Wood can see both sides of any issue, and is best able to serve as interpreter for the Water/Earth combination.

Wood/Metal

Metal can fell Wood with one quick chop if the energy is destructive. Metal ideology and natural genius make Wood feel inadequate and ill-equipped to deal with Metal's solitary nature and at times there will seem to be absolutely no basis for real understanding here. Wood must use its expansiveness to stay one step ahead of Metal. If Wood cannot charm Metal with the newest ideas, then he can take advantage of Metal's tendency to tunnel vision by expanding in other directions, outside of the realm of Metal's influence. Above all, Wood must remember not to attempt to fit the Metal personality into his organization and turn his energies instead to the application of Metal ideas. If he can learn to allow for the peculiarities of Metal, and allow him to go his own way, he can surely stay out of the way of Metal's blade.

Earth/Wood

Even the seemingly inexhaustible energy of Earth can be severely depleted by Wood's energetic demands upon its resources. In a situation of this kind, Earth must be careful to take time away from Wood to renew itself according to the rhythms of nature. Earth has a natural tendency to lend its support to any number of Wood enterprises, and can allow himself to be utterly exploited if he is not careful to manage his own energy wisely. Earth must ignore, upon occasion, its tendency to nurture. Too much support for Wood in this case only serves to expand Wood in all directions and create more problems than it will ever solve. In a word, it is Earth's task in this situation to, upon occasion, "just say no."

Chapter Six

BALANCING
YOUR ELEMENTS

In the best of all possible worlds, each of the Five
Elements is represented in the fortunate person's
elemental birth chart. The presence of all elements in the chart provides resilience, regenera-
tion, a balanced outlook, and protection from the
destructive aspects of any one element. Most people, however, lack at least one or two of the Five
Elements and have a preponderance of others.

The Chinese solved this problem by adding any
missing elements to the name of the individual in
the form of words. Every name was classified according to the Five Elements, and drawn to balance the birth chart. Written, Chinese is a picture
language, brush strokes are used to draw a picto-
gram of each word, and specific numbers of strokes
are assigned to each element. Missing Wood is
added to a personality by including one- or two-
stroke words, Fire by three- or four-stroke words,
Earth by five- or six-stroke words, Metal by a

seven- or eight-stroke word, and Water by a nine-
or ten-stroke word.

Obviously, adding characters or strokes to the
writing of one's name is impractical for Westerners,
but the philosophical base for such a practice remains valid. In this chapter, we explore varieties
of ways in which you can add complementary
elements and influences to your life, using the
methods and practices proscribed by Chinese astrology's sister science of geomancy, Feng Shui.
For a more thorough understanding of how this
system works, we advise you consult several of the
excellent Feng Shui books available on the market.

Feng Shui is the Chinese Art of Placement. According to geomantic theory, the Earth is criss-
crossed by energy lines that form an invisible grid
across its surface. That energy can be tapped and
circulated in constructive ways through the environment in order to augment and combine the
elemental characteristics of families, individuals,
and businesses. Feng Shui is a complicated practice and is most effective when the advice of a
Feng Shui master is followed.

Just as the Earth's energy can be channeled to
enhance any environment according to the principles of the Five Elements, so the energy of the
individual can be enhanced and balanced by putting the same principles to work in one's living
environment, personal adornment, choice of friends, occupation, and recreational activities.

In the following easy reference table, we have
included each of the five elements, followed by

their ruling colors, corresponding occupations, careers, personal talismans, and natural environments. In augmenting your elemental balance, refer to this table for some suggestions. For example, a Metal-dominated individual would want to balance himself with objects or colors that would, in effect, add the influences of Wood, Water, FIre, and Earth.

TABLE 6-1: AUGMENTING YOUR ELEMENTS

ELEMENT	COLOR	TALISMAN	ENVIRONMENT	BUSINESS
Metal	White	Gold	Urban	Aerospace, Mining
Water	Black	Aquarium	Near Water	Counseling, Communications
Wood	Green/Blue	Plants	Forest/country	Architecture, Paper products
Fire	Red	Candles	City	Politics, Theater, Performing
Earth	Yellow	Gemstones	Farmland	Real estate, Property, Finance

Correcting Your Elemental Imbalance

The Metal Personality

A person with a preponderance of Metal in his chart, depending on what other elements are present in the chart as a whole, must begin by adding those elements that are missing altogether. Always remember to adapt according to the specific elemental variations in your chart. A Metal/Fire personality is not the same as someone dominated completely by the Metal element. For instance, if you are a Metal/Fire combination, you do not need to be as cautious about associations with Fire personalities as a Metal/Wood person might be. You may also become successful in Fire careers, which would normally be detrimental to Metal.

To begin with, perhaps the easiest thing a Metal person can do to balance out his element is to get out and make friends with Wood-, Water-, and Earth-dominant types. Once he has established a network of associations and made the necessary adjustments in his environment, he can begin to associate with Fire personalities, (normally destructive to Metal), but he should proceed with caution until his missing Fire has been balanced by other factors.

To balance missing elements, the Metal-dominated personality should begin by avoiding those things that will only serve to reinforce Metal energy. In personal dress and interior decor, a Metal-dominated person should try to avoid white, even though he is drawn to this color. He should also attempt to avoid wearing gold or silver jewelry, Instead, coral, jade, sodalite, or lapis (all related to elemental Earth) can help him to be more practical and serene.

The Metal-dominated individual can augment missing Wood by wearing wooden bracelets or charms to make up for the missing element. Houseplants are also Wood-related, and if he places a plant just inside his front door, one at the far left corner of his living room, and one at the far left corner of his bedroom, he will be able to channel his creativity into practical, enterprising activity and expand his circle of friends and associates with Wood-style sociability. It will also help if he can surround himself at work and at home with natural objects. Decorative seashells serve to augment both missing Water and Wood; fossils and stones augment missing Earth. So surrounded, he will respond positively to difficult situations and be able to maintain an optimistic point of view, rather than submerging himself in Metal-induced bouts of depression.

A Metal-dominated person would do well to include green and black in his interior and personal dress. Green, the ruling color of Wood, helps him to be more practical in his visionary schemes. Black, Water's ruling color, helps him to communicate more effectively with others. The Metal-dominated should live in an urban area surrounded by water, build his home on the shore of a large river or lake, or choose a location dotted with streams and waterfalls. If he can't live or work within view of water, he should install a fish tank or aquarium in his office and his home. Water's influence will make him more empathetic and flexible and serve to increase his profits and social contacts.

Missing Fire can be added to this personality by carrying a hand mirror in his pocket or bag and making use of candles in his home to enhance his relaxation. Fireplaces are also effective. Another way to add Fire is through the use of the color red somewhere in the home, office, or in personal dress. Finally, the missing Fire can also be added to the personality by doing breath exercises, which can be learned from Yogic or T'ai Chi disciplines.

Missing Earth can be integrated by wearing warm-colored gemstones and using large crystals as decoration. Terrariums are also effective; these will serve to calm and stabilize the Metal personality as well as make him more generous and patient with others. He will also be more inclined to support worthy causes with his financial gains.

Depending on the makeup of the chart, a Metal personality does well in Wood or Water industries such as forestry, architecture, woodworking and design, paper products, counseling, publishing or communcations. In addition, this individual also does well in any Metal-associated industry—mining, automobiles, airplane, and train manufacture, food preservation, metal sculpture, wrought iron and decorative Metal arts and jewelry. They also excel in speculation in foreign currency. But they will not necessarily find success in the Fire-ruled professions of drama and politics or the Earth-ruled professions of real estate and property speculation. Earth-type executive positions may not appeal to them, either. Metal-dominated people can be unusually effective in electronics, computers, and television, if they make sure to get the proper amounts of rest and relaxation. All that electrical input can fray the Metal personality's nerves. The strong regenerative powers of Metal make them excellent healers, both physically and mentally, because they can assume the detachment necessary for dealing with those who are in pain.

Metal people need to physically burn off their excess mental energy and would do well to distribute pooled brain energy throughout their bodies. Recreational pursuits can include boating, gardening, and walking. Yoga and meditative exercise like T'ai Chi are also beneficial because they help to circulate energy throughout the Metal person's body. A Metal-dominated person has amazing recuperative powers if he can maintain his calm and balance his internal energy.

If you are a Metal person, you will know that the Metal in your chart has been properly balanced when you find yourself choosing your words wisely and well. Your thoughts will not be scattered or obtuse. You will note that your visionary ideas now have the ability to inspire others, rather than confuse them. In addition, you will be able to listen to others calmly and offer advice that is fair and uncolored by your own judgments or the way you believe things should be in a perfect world. You will be able to verbalize your thoughts in a self-confident manner, and you will be more open to others, generally happier, and possessed of greater social and professional skills.

The Water Personality

Those with an overabundance of Water will want to balance their natures by adding Metal, Wood, and Fire to their personal and professional environments and, to a somewhat lesser extent, Earth. Dominant Water personalities tend to be one of two types: those who rush around and don't accomplish anything or repeat the same tasks over and over, and those who have the characteristics of the stagnant pond, so enervated that they can't move a muscle. If uncorrected, these will become isolated and underachieving. It is likely that many agoraphobics have an overabundance of Water of this latter type.

It is recommended that anyone who lacks specific elements should begin by making friends and associates who are dominated by the elements they lack. The sympathetic Water-dominated individual should find it easy to extend his personal contacts to include people with dominant Metal, Fire, and Wood rather than associating solely with other Water-dominant types. They should take care when introducing Earth people into their lives, doing so gradually, because Earth can absorb Water energy. When Water enters into relationships with Earth personalities, they should be sure to have extra Wood around in case they run into trouble. Any element augmentation generally takes effect after about a month, although sensitive Water types will be able to notice change almost immediately in the way they feel and act. Remember, Water people are psychic in their response to their surroundings.

Water-dominant personalities wishing to add Metal energy and strength should wear gold jewelry. They will be attracted to the subtlety of silver, but gold provides positive and constructive Metal input without imparting Metal's ability to tune into the psychic, lunar type input that silver attracts. Water has enough intuitive input already. Wearing white and incorporating whites and off-whites into interior decor also augments Metal energy. Although Water personalities are attracted to the color black, they should use it sparingly in dress and decor, because black enhances water characteristics. The color green adds the practical detail-oriented outlook of Wood, always useful to excess Water, who can never quite manage to get things done. When worn or used in decorating, red provides missing Fire, and provides Water with style, flair, and personal assertiveness.

To augment missing Earth, Water would do well to wear red or orange gemstones set in gold. Carnelians are an excellent choice. These stones help the Water person refrain from a tendency to complain or manipulate others into feeling sorry for them. Carnelians lend self-reliance, stability, and logic to the impressionable Water personality. Such ornaments help Water to intellectualize his problems and not take everything so personally. Earth-based crystals and gemstones also give Water the necessary stamina to see a project through to completion. Bowls of attractively displayed agates or crystals can be placed in Water's living and working areas to achieve the same goal.

Missing Fire can be augmented by the use of candles or a night-light in Water's sleeping area. Fire attributes are absorbed subconsciously by the Water dominant. To a lesser extent, the Water person can also incorporate missing Fire by attending theatrical events, large, sophisticated parties, or by volunteering for political work, and will find such activities highly stimulating. Carrying a hand mirror or cigarette lighter is also effective.

People who have an abundance of rushing Water can spend a few moments upon waking each morning to quiet and clear their minds before the day begins. Such brief meditations aid in breaking counterproductive patterns of repeated behaviors. People with an excess of still water, unable to motivate themselves to get out of the house, can select two or three new people to contact or things to do each day. It is important that this be done without Water complaining or feeling sorry for himself. Water is also advised to participate in adult education programs and the arts.

Water does well professionally when involved in the Wood industries associated with paper products, forestry, and things constructed of Wood. It excels in its own Water-related businesses of counseling, therapy, public relations, teaching, communications, and public speaking. Fire-governed industries such as publicity, drama, entertainment, and politics also aid the somewhat introverted

Water-based person and serve to draw him out. Water dominant people should avoid Metal- and Earth-ruled industries, because they are likely to find them too restrictive, demanding, and generally strenuous for their sensitive natures.

Recreational pursuits that benefit Water are swimming, boating, scuba diving, and other Water-related activities. Water people need to guard against nervousness and stress and will find that such pursuits have a calming, beneficial effect on their psyches. Water people also enjoy all types of socializing. If mild exercise can be combined with social contact, in dancing, for example, so much the better. Water people must be careful to avoid strenuous exercise—overexertion or highly competitive sports will prove too stressful for Water types. Yoga, meditation, music, and art classes are wonderful recreations for Water personalities.

The Water personality will know he is balanced when he is able to flow without being diverted or distracted by obstacles. Balanced Water will be able to accomplish goals in a timely manner and be able to extend help and support to those around him without getting bogged down in the problems and emotions of others. Properly aligned, Water energy is powerful, able to take an active part in things and flexible without being passive. Even a still-water type is highly intelligent, meditative, and able to communicate his insights and observations in constructive ways, uncolored by excess of emotionalism, fearfulness, and hypersensitivty.

The Wood Personality

Dominant Wood, like Water, needs to learn to finish what it starts. Unlike Water, however, those who are dominated by the element of Wood need, more than any other type, to empathize with others and to expand and develop in the area of personal relationships. They can learn much from Water associates in this, particularly when it comes to personal communications. The Fire personality draws the Wood type out, and Earth teaches him to be more caring. When the Wood-dominated personality has developed associates and friends in each of the preceding elements, he will be able to form relationships with Metal-dominated types without fear of exploitation or destruction.

To incorporate missing Water, the Wood personality should try to establish his home or place of business within view of a body of water, or fountain. Curiously, however, the Wood personality should avoid positioning himself near any sluggish or polluted river or pond, because this can have an adverse effect on his ethical code in business dealings. Failing water visibility, though, he can install an aquarium in his home or office or, at the very least, be sure to keep clear glass vases filled with water and flowers near him. Water serves to stimulate Wood's financial success, improves his communications with others, and provides him with greater sensitivity to the arts and the creative side of life.

Although Wood is doubtless attracted to green and blue, his ruling colors, he should try to avoid them in personal dress and decor and augment his missing elements with black for Water, yellow for Earth, red for Fire, and whites and off-whites for Metal. Red adds sophistication to Wood and impart Fire's flair. Yellow balances Wood's obsession with newness and expansion and improves his discernment, and Black makes him more sensitive.

Missing Fire can be included by adding a fireplace to the home, serving to improve Wood's family relationships. Dining by candlelight serves to stimulate lively discussion and social interaction. If they can tear themselves away from their hectic and demanding schedules, Wood people can also incorporate missing Fire by attending theatrical and performing events, or getting involved in community politics. In order for this to be truly effective, though, they have to make an effort to take these pleasures on their own terms, and not use such occasions simply to further their business networks.

Missing Earth can be augmented by carrying light stones or talismans made of amber (a Wood/Earth combination). Paintings or artwork depicting natural landscapes or wildlife help to stabilize Wood's tendency to overexpand and overextend himself. Taking time to garden, landscape, or just get outdoors and get his hands dirty will also help the Wood personality to keep in touch with Earth's stabilizing influences. Small stone sculptures of jade, coral, or stone can be added in the office or at home to help improve Wood concentration. The addition of Earth in any form enables Wood to express his natural kindness and concern for others in practical ways, rather than in grandiose theories and designs.

In the destructive cycle, Metal can be injurious to Wood, and its incorporation should be handled with care and discrimination. Silver and gold jewelry are excellent choices for Metal augmentation and can do much to contribute to Wood intellect and insight. Computers and electronic gadgets are beneficial to Wood enterprises, although he may never quite get the hang of the gadgetry himself. Metal sculpture and furniture can also be added, but it should never be large or overpowering. Placing Metal objects near stairwells or entries should also be strictly avoided, because it is likely to cause mishaps or injuries. Especially avoid freestanding metal spiral staircases—for Wood, this is an accident waiting to happen.

If there are plants or plantings in a Wood environment, it is important that they be well cared for and kept healthy at all times. Dead or dying plants are detrimental to the Wood psyche and are a drain on his energy.

Wood people live to work, and they are highly successful in Earth-related industries, such as real estate, agriculture, restaurants, or finance. Wood-ruled professions like forestry, architecture, and adminstrative positions of all kinds are well suited to him, as are the Water-ruled vocations of communications or arts administration. He may not be quite so successful in more personal types of Water professions—counseling, for example—and he should be cautious about Fire professions as well. In Metal-ruled professions, he is almost sure to take a beating, unless there are mitigating circumstances in his chart or in the work force and associates.

Wood people thrive on recreational pursuits that involve the great outdoors. Camping, canoeing, gardening, white-water rafting, and even mountain-climbing and hiking stimulate and challenge him. Artistic pursuits will improve his sensitivity and he might excel in applied, rather than fine arts. Sculpture is another excellent choice, as long as it is not metalworking, and he enjoys furniture restoration and building that weekend getaway. He will doubtless be happiest with a country place to which he can retreat and separate himself from the demands of the Wood lifestyle.

A balanced Wood personality is receptive to new ideas but not overcome or distracted by them. He will use his strong ethical sense and will incorporate innovation into his efficient administrative system. The balanced Wood personality allows for loners and dissidents and does not constantly strive to push them into his organization. On the other hand, he is able to make his own decisions and not find himself so easily swayed by the opinions and advice of others. He does not overextend himself, nor does he get caught up in a plethora of detail. It is easier for him to execute his plans and ideas, and he is careful to finish what he starts.

The Fire Personality

Those who have a preponderance of Fire in their birth charts do well to build steadfastness, endurance, and consideration for others. Associations with Wood, Metal, and Earth types certainly benefit them in these areas, but, like all other elements, they must take care when entering into relationships with the element capable of destroying or depleting their own. In this case, Fire must approach Water cautiously, and be careful not to underestimate the power of Water energy. Water's emotionalism has a tendency to depress Fire and to destroy his passion and enthusiasm. Balanced by other associations, though, Water friends can be absorbed by the Fire personality without undue strain on anyone.

The Fire-dominated personality can incorporate missing Wood by adding plants, though he will have to remember to water them occasionally. (Fire is notorious for neglecting that kind of detail.) Art objects of petrified wood, wood sculptures, or a living space with lots of woodwork will also serve the purpose. Wooden beads, belt buckles, bracelets, and other personal ornaments help to render excess Fire more cooperative and patient, and enable him to devote more of his talents to administrative, rather than starring roles in his areas of endeavor. Fire can prosper by living in wooded areas. The daily influence of Wood alleviates Fire's tendency to cruelty and those fiery fits of temper brought on by frustration.

Missing Metal can be integrated in any number of ways. Fire delights in extravagant gold and silver jewelry, avant-garde metal sculpture, decorative metalwork, and metal embellishments of all kinds. A display of exotic coins or weaponry also suits the Fire personality. Fire people are probably the only people in the world who can incorporate a giant brass gong into their home or office decor and make it work. Metal helps Fire's concentration and serves to foster his creativity and intuition. Metal helps to draw the new ideas Fire needs to fuel his passions, and imparts a degree of emotional independence.

Missing Earth can be added to Fire's environment through stone sculpture—small statues are best, preferably set outdoors in gardens or wooded groves. Too much stone will depress Fire and dampen his enthusiasm. His is not a personality that responds well to monuments or monoliths. Fire, however, reacts quite happily to Earth-ruled gemstones in fiery colors—rubies, garnets, and yellow topaz are most effective. Earth's influence mitigates Fire's self-destructive tendencies, and imparts a degree of stick-to-it-iveness that otherwise might be lacking. Earth's influence adds to Fire's intelligence and improves his discrimination, steering Fire away from his tendency to grandstand and into areas where he can burn more serenely and comfortably—assuming more the character of a fireplace than a conflagration. Both Earth and Wood do much for Fire, imparting practicality, patience, and attention to detail.

Water can be incorporated by the use of small reflecting ponds or aquariums stocked with red, yellow, and orange fish. However, Fire-dominated individuals should remember to take their Water energy in small doses. They would rather live next to a foundry than have oceanfront property; the sound of the waves that others find so soothing drives them to distraction with its relentless pounding. Still, Water can aid in developing Fire's intuitive nature and make him less self-involved.

The restlessness of Fire is reported to be much improved when their beds, desks, homes, or offices face south, Fire's natural direction. Such placement aids in stabilizing their tempers and helps in relaxation.

Fire does well professionally when he is in the limelight. Celebrity is possibly the best choice for Fire types, but because that is not always possible, there are quite a few other areas he can pursue with great success. Entertainment industries are always well suited to Fire personalities, as are the many types of broadcasting, electronics, and the military. He may be an excellent club owner or restaurateur, providing he can delegate certain responsibilities—turning the menu over to an Earth personality and the bar over to a Water type, for example. His inspirational qualities make him well suited to both politics and religion, though he will do well in both instances to surround himself with the high ethics of Wood and the natural caution of Earth. In positions of power, he will do well to limit his Water associates, because their penchant for intrigue could undermine his efforts. Equally, the Fire personality succeeds in Metal- or Wood-ruled industries. He should steer clear of counseling or teaching vocations because he lacks the necessary patience; banking, real estate, and farming bore him to tears.

Recreationally, the Fire personality is well suited to highly competitive sports, and in some cases, even dangerous ones. Race-car driving, demolition derbys, competitive fencing—as long as there is a degree of danger and plenty of spectators, the Fire personality will have the time of his life. He should keep his daredevil activities out of the Water, however. Water sports can be downright dangerous for this character. He enjoys art and related events, and if he can relieve himself of the continual need to be center stage, an occasional turn around a museum will broaden his perspectives and objectivity. Any classes involving meditation and breathing techniques also benefit the Fire personality, because they allow him to let off the necessary steam.

Well balanced, the Fire personality is the embodiment of reason and impeccable behavior. His social skills are sophisticated while remaining characteristically expressive, and there is less the aura of the loose cannon around this individual. Fire cruelty is kept in check when balanced, and his criticism is astute, well-considered, and effective. He shows greater tolerance of others, is considerate of their feelings, and is able to control his anger and impatience. In short, the balanced Fire personality can be a guiding light to all he meets.

The Earth Personality

Although truly Earth-dominated personalities are somewhat rare, even two Earth aspects can impart a distinctly Earthbound quality to the individual chart. Earth people do well to form immediate and lasting associations with Metal and Water types, who will inspire their natural capabilities, broaden their social and professional relationships, and keep them from getting into those comfortable ruts to which Earth-dominated people are prone. Both types also stimulate Earth's imagination, without paralyzing his conservative nature. When Earth adds Fire to his circle of friends, it serves to add to his sophistication and social flair, and enables Earth to extend himself with greater confidence. Earth should, however, be careful to balance himself with other elements before proceeding into a relationship with a Wood personality; Wood is capable of depleting Earth's energy.

Missing Water can be incorporated into Earth's environment by living within sight of rivers, ponds, and streams, as well as waterfalls and oceans. He should avoid marshy or stagnant areas. Earth people are happiest in rural or suburban environments, but if forced to dwell in urban areas, they can incorporate Water's influence through the use of aquariums or fountains. Earth appreciates the soothing qualities of Water and responds to Water's influence in increased sensitivity and sociability. Under Water's influence, Earth can learn to express itself more easily, and communicate some of those deeply felt emotions. Water's influence makes Earth more recepetive to subtle influences and more flexible in his dealings with others.

The Earth person can add missing Metal by wearing modest gold or silver jewelry (the investment value will appeal to him), or by incorporating metal objects (antiques are particularly suited to Earth personalities) in living and working spaces. Metal inspires Earth and stimulates his intellectual and creative abilities. Electronic gadgets and sound systems are also effective—they provide Earth with access to the world of ideas through broadcasts. In addition, all Earth types love the sensuality and comfort of good music. Metal impulses conduct Earth's regenerative powers quickly to those around him, and also protect Earth against an excess of philanthropy.

Fire can be augmented by carrying a small mirror. Earth can also augment the Fire element in the home by installing fireplaces (preferably stone), which will subdue Fire's effect. Earth is comforted by the optimistic influences of Fire, and candle-light also appeals to his sensual side. Earth is cheered and energized by Fire's influence as long as it is kept firmly under control. Excessive Fire turns him stubborn and determined to have his own way.

Wood influence should be added sparingly, preferably through the use of small houseplants in living areas and herb pots or windowboxes in the kitchen. Outdoors, Wood influence can be added by covering lawns with creeping groundcover such as chamomile or English ivy. Earth has great sympathy for Wood energy and any dying or wilting plant should be removed immediately so as to avoid an energy drain. Earth-dominated farmers or agriculturalists are equally affected by ailing or failing crops. It is only their great reserves of strength and belief in regenerative cycles that enable them to endure through such seasons.

White, black, and red bring prosperity to Earth businesses. Such a combination has popular appeal, certainly important in Earth-ruled pursuits like cozy little restaurants. The Earth personality excels in businesses like agriculture, food service, restaurants, hotel management, real estate, and finance. They can also excel in Metal-related professions like auto companies, aircraft, mining, jewelry making, machinery, and electronics if they are allowed to be the brains behind the operation. They prosper in the Water-related fields of the arts, ocean commerce, and the humanities. Many will consider Fire-related businesses if they are allowed to participate in them in a behind-the-scenes capacity as agents or producers. Wood industries will only drain Earth's energies and resources. The Earth personality, whatever his chosen field, excels in top and middle management.

Earth types most enjoy leisure time spent in museums or historical sites. They have a true appreciation of antiques, history, and the classics. They enjoy those things that endure. Artistically inclined Earth types respond well to crafts such as pottery, ceramics, and clay sculpture. Whatever their choice, their recreational environments must be traditional, solid, and elegant. They doubtless enjoy any activities involving gardening (the Earth garden will be immense and profuse) and boating, although they will be more inclined to take luxurious cruises than sailing solo around the world. Earth's great physical strength adores hiking, riding, spelunking, and mountaineering. Earth sports will be those requiring stamina and endurance. Earth types enjoy small dinner parties and cooking for their friends. They can find outlets for their energies in social work and neighborhood activities, and their sensuality and natural rhythm makes them terrific dancers.

Well-balanced Earth people are considerate of others, reliable, and loyal without being inflexible or stodgy. They are responsible when handling the resources of others and are able to share without depleting themselves. They may not say much, but their words are wise and sympathetic. They eventually realize that there is more to life than self-reliance, and their innate fear of change will be mitigated by an enjoyment of new ideas and innovations.

BIBLIOGRAPHY

Ming-Shui, The Art and Practice of Chinese Astrology, Derek Walters. Pagoda Books, S. S. Fireside reprint, London, 1987.

Chinese Beliefs and Superstitions, Evelyn Lip. Graham Brash Ltd., Singapore, 1985.

The Encyclopedia of Fortunetelling, Francis X. King. W. H. Smith, New York, 1988.

Interior Design with Fèng Shui, Sarah Rossbach. E. P. Dutton, New York, 1987.

The Healing Tao, Mantak Chia and Maneewuan Chia. The Healing Tao Center, New York, 1983.

The Handbook of Chinese Horoscopes, Theodore Lau. Harper & Row, New York, 1979.

The I Ching, Wilhelm-Baynes. Princeton University Press, New Jersey, 1950.

Iron Shirt Chi Kung I, Mantak Chia. Healing Tao Books, New York, 1986.

The Book of Macrobiotics, Michio Kushi. Japan Publications, Tokyo, 1977.

By the year 2000, 2 out of 3 Americans could be illiterate.

It's true.

Today, 75 million adults...about one American in three, can't read adequately. And by the year 2000, U.S. News & World Report envisions an America with a literacy rate of only 30%.

Before that America comes to be, you can stop it...by joining the fight against illiteracy today.

Call the Coalition for Literacy at toll-free **1-800-228-8813** and volunteer.

Volunteer Against Illiteracy.
The only degree you need is a degree of caring.

THIS AD PRODUCED BY MARTIN LITHOGRAPHERS
A MARTIN COMMUNICATIONS COMPANY